I0029230

THE THEORY OF LEGAL SCIENCE

THE THEORY

OF

LEGAL SCIENCE

BY HUNTINGTON CAIRNS

CHAPEL HILL · 1941

The University of North Carolina Press

COPYRIGHT, 1941, BY

THE UNIVERSITY OF NORTH CAROLINA PRESS

DESIGNED BY STEFAN SALTER

ACKNOWLEDGMENT

Portions of this book have appeared in the *Columbia Law Review,* the *Iowa Law Review,* and the *Philosophy of Science Journal.* Grateful acknowledgment is made to the editors of those journals for their kind permission to reprint.

CONTENTS

This whole book is but a draught—nay, but the draught of a draught. Oh, Time, Strength, Cash and Patience!

Herman Melville

1.

THE THEORY OF JURISPRUDENCE

JURISPRUDENCE AS HERE CONCEIVED may be defined provisionally as the study of human behavior as a function of disorder.
All the social sciences study human activity, but, as we are becoming increasingly aware, each studies it as a function of, or
as influenced by, a particular factor or set of factors. Human
geography, for example, takes as its field human behavior in
relation to the phenomena of physical geography, and economics as conceived by an acute modern thinker is concerned
with that aspect of human conduct imposed by the influence
of scarcity.[1] All theories of society, it is important to recognize
at the outset, must begin with certain unprovable assumptions;
it is impossible to test them conclusively by experimental or
formal means. All that we may do is to state why they appear
valid to us, and why opposing notions either are invalid or inadequate for the task in hand. Such is the situation here. Human behavior as the object of study of jurisprudence presents
no real difficulty. This aspect of the suggested view of jurisprudence is exclusively a matter of definition. We look at all
the social sciences and observe that they all study human be-

[1] Brunhes, *Human Geography*, in Barnes (ed.), *History and Prospects
of the Social Sciences* (1925) 55; Robbins, *An Essay on the Nature and
Significance of Economic Science* (2nd ed., 1935) 16.

havior but from different focal points. The social sciences therefore may be defined as the group of sciences concerned with the study of human behavior as it manifests itself in social action. It follows then that jurisprudence, if aspiring to the rank of a social science, must similarly have, as its object of study, human behavior.

We encounter difficulties when we attempt to isolate the factor or set of factors in relation to which human behavior should be analyzed by jurisprudence. It is here that we must rest upon assumptions. The idea that "disorder" is the required factor is based upon several ultimate beliefs. The first of these is that order is a necessary element in all societary accomplishment; it is certainly a characteristic of all societies. Accomplishment is used here in a broad sense and includes such primary ends as the mere preservation of existence. Anthropology has revealed to us no society which does not possess a social structure and which does not disclose a sequence or arrangement of activities, individual and group, for the realization of certain ends. The second assumption is that the primary objective of purposive control is the achievement of societary order. The elimination of disorder is the principal task of social control, and it is human behavior as a function of disorder which would seem, in its broadest aspects, to be the province of jurisprudence. "Disorder" appears to be the general element in the situation and, at the same time, the most fruitful for a social science jurisprudence. Under the influence of economic thought, Roscoe Pound has found the ultimate basis of his engineering interpretation of the legal process in the notion of scarcity.[2] His theory is "that there are not enough of the material goods of existence . . . to go round; that while individual claims and wants and desires are infinite, the material means of satisfying them are finite. . . . Thus we may think of the task of the legal order as one . . . of conserving the goods of existence in order to make them go as far as possible, and of precluding friction and eliminating waste in the human use and enjoyment of

[2] *The Spirit of the Common Law* (1925) 196.

them." This conception overlooks the fact that scarcity is only one of the many factors producing disorder: if there were enough of the material goods to go round, scarcity would cease to be even one of the factors contributing to disorder; war, pestilence, sex hunger, selfishness, all may, and frequently do, lead to social disorder. The general societal element is disorder and not scarcity. Similarly, while it is true that order in society is achieved by delimiting the interests, desires and demands of its individual members, order is the primary, and interests and desires and demands the secondary element. Order is the constant, and interests, desires and demands the variables. They are delimited to insure order; and by the achievement of order they are thereby made more secure.

Jurisprudence is customarily defined as the science of law. This definition intellectually is on a level with the archaic definition of economics as the science of wealth. It expresses no clear point of view, indicates no problem, describes no subject matter, and is incapable of generalization. Above all, it is inadequate for the purposes of a social science jurisprudence, the subject to be studied here. This subject, as Bertrand Russell once remarked of the science of pure mathematics, was baptized long before it was born. Students of jurisprudence, in American legal circles at all events, have long since appropriated to their studies the label "social science." Generally, however, they have been content with acceptance of the honorific connotations of the term; however valuable their researches may be in the task of elucidating the legal process, and however much such researches may be utilized in the ultimate establishment of jurisprudence as a social science, it should be plain that modern legal study, with few exceptions, possesses none of the characteristics of social science.

As it stands provisionally the conception of jurisprudence as the study of human behavior as a function of disorder embraces a field considerably larger than that customarily conceived to be within its province. It obviously includes a large part at least of the subject matter of political science.

No doubt it is desirable to delimit the two fields, but at the present stage, at any rate, this is impossible. Much of the subject matter included within the domain of political science seems to be essential to a general theory of law. In the past the provinces of jurisprudence and political science have never been separated satisfactorily and it is not improbable that with the development of jurisprudence as a social science the task will be found to be impossible, at least as political science is currently understood. Divisions among the sciences are artificial and not necessary; their chief function is as an aid to research by directing attention to specific fields of study.

PRESENT-DAY AMERICAN LEGAL THOUGHT

At this point it will be helpful if we glance briefly at the salient characteristics of modern American legal thought. Legal thinking is no exception to the general rule that the distinctive characteristics, even the choice of subject matter, of many domains of thought are determined by their first assumptions. Maine's [3] conviction that civilization is a rare exception in world history, and that Rousseau's doctrine of natural rights was inimical to its continued existence, fixed the general character of his theory of law and government and influenced the selection of the problems he chose to investigate. Brooks Adams' [4] materialist conception of history led him inevitably to the conclusion that the law's content is the product of the self-interest of successive dominant classes. So it is with other legal thinkers and with other schools of legal thought. Fundamental opinions in law and the social sciences, however the case may be with some at least

[3] *Ancient Law* (World's Classics ed., 1931) 18; *Popular Government* (1886) 75, 134, 143, 152-54 and *passim*.

[4] *Centralization and the Law* (1906) 63-64; *The Modern Conception of Animus* (1907) 19 Green Bag 12.

of the natural sciences, possess a special importance; it is well to pause from time to time to take stock of them.

Underlying the investigations of modern legal research is the conviction that such research can be made beneficial to the administration of justice; it is equally an assumption of the sociological jurists,[5] the realists [6] and the newborn experimental jurists.[7] Perhaps this conviction came into legal thought partly as a result of the contempt in which jurisprudence was held by the legal profession of the Nineteenth Century. "Jurisprudence," said Dicey in an often quoted remark, "stinks in the nostrils of the practising barrister." It would be an adequate answer to the practising barrister, however, and one which would effectively silence him, if it were pointed out that legal research—not in the sense of mere historical investigation, but in the sense of a complete analysis of "law in action"—was being undertaken for the purposes of law reform and not with the aim of inventing another game similar to the entertaining one with which the analytical jurists amused themselves a generation or two ago. Perhaps also the conviction became a part of legal thought as the outcome of the endless stream of criticism directed by social scientists at the actual administration of justice. There seemed indeed to be a prevalent opinion that law could never become a social science unless something were done with respect to the improvement of the administration of justice, although it never occurred to anyone to suggest that economics could never attain the status of a social science unless it corrected the much worse state of affairs obtaining in its field. Perhaps this underlying assumption can also be accounted for by the

[5] Pound, *Interpretations of Legal History* (1923) 151-65; *idem, Criminal Justice in America* (1930) 211-12; *idem, The Spirit of the Common Law* (1921) 212-15; *idem, art., Jurisprudence,* in Gee (ed.), *Research in the Social Sciences* (1929) 181.

[6] Llewellyn, *The Conditions for and the Aims and Methods of Legal Research,* Am. L. School Rev. (March, 1930) 672.

[7] Beutel, *Some Implications of Experimental Jurisprudence* (1934) 48 Harv. L. Rev. 169.

simple fact that legal students here recognized a profitable field of research. Whatever may be its explanation, it is indubitably an essential part of contemporary legal thinking and it has had an unequivocal effect upon the aims and methods of contemporary legal research.

It has had its deepest influence in the selection of the subject matter for investigation. This subject matter in its broadest terms may be denominated "law in action." Each school approaches this field from the standpoint of its own special conceptions but its program rarely exceeds the limits marked out by the subject matter "law in action." The program of the sociological school, formulated by Pound,[8] insists upon eight points: (1) Study of the actual social effects of legal institutions, legal precepts, and legal doctrines; (2) Sociological study in preparation for law-making; (3) Study of the means of making legal precepts effective in action; (4) Study of juridical action; (5) A sociological legal history; (6) Recognition of the importance of individualized application of legal precepts—of reasonable and just solutions of individual cases; (7) In English-speaking countries, a Ministry of Justice; and (8) That the end of juristic study, toward which the foregoing are but some of the means, is to make effort more effective in achieving the purposes of law. Llewellyn[9] has similarly, but less systematically, marked out for the realists their domain of study. He thinks that the immediate aim of legal research ought to be, and probably for the next ten years will be, the "checking up on the effects of the law in life . . . first, for the purpose of discovering what the rules really are and mean; second, for the purpose of utilizing them and planning their utilization; third, for the purpose of criticizing them and preparing a way for law reform; and, lastly, as the indispensable basis for any pure legal science which deserves the name." An ambitious program for the so-called

[8] *Outlines of Lectures on Jurisprudence* (4th ed., 1928) 16-18.
[9] *Op. cit. supra* note 6 at 674. Cf. *idem, A Realistic Jurisprudence—The Next Step* (1930) 30 Col. L. Rev. 431.

experimental jurists has been stated recently by Beutel.[10] This school's primary object is to discover, with the assistance of an instrument—the experimental method—which they hope will yield more precise results than those obtained in the past, the extent to which law reform is necessary and how it should be accomplished. The programs of all these schools have in common fundamentally the same subject matter—law in action; and it is apparent that the selection of that subject matter in the first instance was determined in large part by the initial assumption that legal research might be profitable for the administration of justice.

A rationalization and defense of the characteristics of modern legal thought has been put forward by Professor Yntema,[11] who declares that the objective analysis of the legal system for the purpose of reform constitutes the "Copernican discovery of modern legal science." His purpose is to show the scientific legitimacy of the subject matter, the necessity for such an objective investigation, and the probability of the realization of fruitful results. He concludes "that such a study of law in action is an essential, if not under present conditions the most essential, object of a legal science which is not to remain esoteric."

JURISPRUDENCE AS A SOCIAL SCIENCE

It requires little reflection, however, to realize that the characteristics exhibited by modern legal study are not characteristics of the principal social sciences. Contemporary legal study is a technology; but the social sciences are not technologies. Their ideal, like the ideal of those departments of knowledge commonly denominated the "natural sciences," is the discovery of general laws which unite a number of particular facts. We may pass over the circumstance that the successes of the social sciences in formulating laws have been

[10] Op. cit. supra note 7.
[11] Legal Science and Reform (1934) 34 Col. L. Rev. 207.

relatively few in number. The ideal remains warranted in the absence of a demonstration—which is still to be offered—that its realization is impossible. Moreover, the fact that the social sciences have put forward some "general laws" which appear to be "true" with respect to the subject matter for which they were framed, is a positive indication that the ideal is permissible. The ideals of the technologies are, however, entirely different and vary from one technology to another. In the case of modern legal study, it is, as we have seen, law reform. It seems scarcely necessary to point out that this difference in ideals is a crucial one. Each ideal determines in large part the subject matter to be selected for examination, the methods to be adopted, even the facts which will be chosen for study. The possibility of legal study as a technology, moreover, raises a special question, one not peculiar to the other studies we know as technologies. It is the characteristic of a technology that it is indebted to many sciences, although it has in many cases its own contribution to make of matter and method. Mechanical engineering, which is beholden to a score or more of sources, is such a subject. This, however, although characteristic, is not always the case; psychology, which until recently was principally concerned with the gathering of facts as a basis for the formulation of general principles or "laws," has now felt that enough of such principles have been formulated to permit it to become also an "applied" science or technology. In its case, psychology is the principal source upon which psychologists draw in making their application. The important point with respect to every technology is, however, that it involves to an exclusive or considerable degree the application of principles or laws formulated by a "pure" science. But this is not the situation in which modern legal study finds itself. It is attempting to be an applied science, although there has been as yet no pure science of law in the sense of a study of the principles governing the relations of law and society. In the absence of such a previous study, the applications of modern legal research must necessarily be of a crude order. They would seem to be confined largely to such problems as the discovery of the manner in which legal procedure should be altered so as to make possible a more expeditious, and at the same time equitable, trial of issues. By its emphasis upon law reform, modern legal study overlooks the fact that it is limiting itself to a circumscribed field of study, and that no matter how successful its accomplishments in this field, it is not a social science nor will it ever become one so long as it maintains its present ideal. More important than these considerations, however, is the fact that modern legal study, by reason of its technological ideal, is overlooking a field of investigation which must be tilled before we can ever have a really fruitful applied legal science. It is the domain which legal research would necessarily explore if it were properly a social science.

Thus, the theory of jurisprudence as a social science marks off a field of inquiry which differs radically from that explored by the major present-day American schools. It differs first in its ideal, which is the ideal of the other social sciences, namely, the formulation of statements asserting invariant, or almost invariant, relationships among the facts in its specific field and, in its special case, the organization of such principles into a coherent system in conjunction with a rational theory of ethics. Secondly, it is concerned with a different subject matter. Its point of departure is not law as such, but human behavior as influenced by, or in relation to, the social factor of disorder. If the attempt is successful to create a jurisprudence which is in actuality a social science, it requires little reflection to grasp the importance of that result. We are living today in a human world which is under reconstruction. The focal point of legal action is shifting; new claims, new demands, are calling for recognition. Our theory of law as we know it now is founded upon a view of a society which is in a rapid state of transformation. It is obvious that the law itself must be modified to meet the forces of the new society. What are the principles which should guide us in that task of modification? In the present state of legal knowledge, we have no better method than that of trial and error. If we were to adopt any of the programs for law reform now urged upon us, we literally do not know whether the effects of those reforms would be beneficial or injurious. In the unlimited extravagance of nature the method of trial and error has proved itself successful; but it is a method too expensive for the limited resources of human society. The earth is peopled with a multitude of living things, but a vaster ill-adapted multitude were doomed to extinction in the fortuitous processes of that experiment. That process, although it is today still the customary one in social action, puts too great a strain upon the delicate balances of society; it is a wasteful method which efficient thought has taught us is within man's power to eliminate. A social science jurisprudence aims at revealing to us the consequences of the various courses of action open to us. It aims to tell us in advance the perils which attend our various programs; to tell us which is the rational and which the irrational course.

That the difficulties in the way of such an achievement are enormous is too plain to require statement. As its end it envisages a completely determinate system, and this no doubt in the social field is many generations short of accomplishment, if indeed it is at all possible. But the attempt to devise or discover such a system possesses in itself an importance not shared by jurisprudence as it is practised today. The problems which the sociological or realistic jurist now studies are suggested in the main by defects in the legal system; reflection is the method which brings them to the surface. The social scientist, however, is working towards a unified theory and the problems which confront him are indicated by the propositions of the system and gaps in the theory. This also saves time and energy. There can be little doubt, to adapt a suggestion of Robbins,[12] that one of the greatest dangers

[12] *Op. cit. supra* note 1 at 3.

which besets the modern jurist is preoccupation with the irrelevant—the multiplication of activities which have little or no connection with the solution of problems strictly germane to his subject. It seems self-evident today that law must be viewed as a social product and not as a self-contained system of knowledge. If the goal of the jurist is a unified theory, that unified theory must be grounded upon social phenomena and not upon legal concepts. The analytical jurist did in fact produce a determinate system but its weakness was that it took very little, if any, account of social phenomena. As such, it failed to meet the needs of common life and if the law had accepted its iron-bound fetters the legal process would have soon become unworkable and intolerable. A science of law based upon an adequate theory of human society concentrates attention upon the principal problems confronting the jurist; their solution, as a consequence, proceeds with greater rapidity. Today relatively little attention is given to those problems at all; instead, the energy of jurists is devoted to tasks which, in their nature, are incapable of solution in the absence of the knowledge sought by social science jurisprudence. Jurisprudence as it is known today is in large part a meaningless and fruitless pursuit of a goal incapable of achievement.

This is not to say that ultimate usefulness should be given weight as a factor in the development of legal theory. At the present time the justification of legal research, if it stands in need of one, is no different from that of the other sciences: it gratifies our intellectual appetites. In this attitude it is no more than assuming the position of the more successful sciences. "Social science," Cohen [13] has written, "can . . . in the long run best attain its goal only when those who cultivate it care more for the scientific game itself and for the meticulous adherence to its rules of evidence than for any of the uses to which their discoveries can be put." It is, indeed, as

[13] *Reason and Nature* (1931) 349.

Titchener [14] observed more than a score of years ago, a distinctive feature of science that it is more rigorous than technology in its observation of the established laws and approved methods of logic; "not," as he was careful to add, "through any superior virtue in the man of science, but simply because the technologist, in the nature of the case, is a logical opportunist, working for results and towards a practical end, and therefore content to work in a logical twilight so long as results are forthcoming and progress can be reported."

Law in action, it should be pointed out, is also within the domain of legal research if human behavior as a function of disorder is taken as its subject matter. Law in action is one aspect of human behavior, and, as such, an element of the social process which must be studied if the relationship of law and society is to be understood in its entirety. Even here, however, the difference in attitude between the investigation of "law in action" as such, and the study of "law in action" in order to relate it to the social process generally, is important. Facts, as Cook [15] has recently emphasized, do not speak for themselves. Their meaning depends to a greater or lesser extent upon the point of view with which we approach them. "The heavens declare the glory of God to one whose mind is kindled with religious zeal," writes Cunningham.[16] "They speak the language of infinite vastness governed by law to the mind fertile in scientific hypotheses; they tell a story of gods and heroes, of loves and antipathies, of births and deaths, to the mind of the romantic poet; they become father, mother, and children, and animals all living a life like our own, to the mind of the myth maker." The facts in the field of "law in action" will speak with one voice to the research student who studies social processes generally, and with a different

[14] *Psychology: Science or Technology* (1914) 84 The Popular Science Monthly 39.

[15] *The Possibilities of Social Study as a Science* in *Essays on Research in the Social Sciences* (1931) 27.

[16] *Textbook of Logic* (1924) 247.

voice to the student whose main concern is law reform.

Jurisprudence can never be satisfied with the mere accumulation of facts, however important those facts in themselves may be. Its object, as a science, must be to ascertain if the complex reality of the phenomena with which it is concerned exhibits elements of orderly recurrence which may be formulated in terms of generalizations or specific laws.

2.

THE SOCIAL BASIS OF LAW

ORDER IS OMNIPRESENT, so far as appears to us, in nature and human thought. At the outset of Western thinking, in the period of early Greek mythology, we encounter the figure of Nemesis, goddess of offended justice, who corrects the inequalities of chance, both in human life and in nature, and who thus assists in maintaining some kind of order in nature. Studies of nest building and the rearing of young birds indicate that they are processes which follow a necessary order. If the order is interrupted it cannot be taken up again at the point of interruption, but a fresh start from the beginning is necessary. An analogous situation is presented when a verse is forgotten and the poem must be repeated from the beginning before the verse is recaptured. In recent experiments, Pavlov has induced profound nervous disturbances in dogs by a change in the order of stimuli.[1] In mathematical and logical thought the idea of order has enormous importance, and in one branch at least, geometry, all the required concepts can be expressed in terms of the concept of order alone. The great Poincaré explained the genius of mathematical creation as an aptitude for the perception of order among elements. In fact, from cosmology to aesthetics the basic theories

[1] Korzybski, *Science and Sanity* (1933) 183.

of most departments of knowledge embrace or rest upon the notion of order.

In social thought, however, customarily it is taken for granted and although its importance frequently is remarked the concept has not been a vital factor. It is true that Hobbes and Comte made it the basis of their systems but such explicit recognitions are rare. Undoubtedly the excessive individualism of Seventeenth and Eighteenth Century thought, with its emphasis on the doctrine of natural rights, accounts, during that period at any rate, for the relative lack of attention given to the theory of social order. In the absence of a civil society, e.g., in a society in which there is no common superior to hold everyone in check, it was held that every man is in the full possession of all his liberties. Upon entering into civil society, however, some "natural rights" are surrendered in order to secure the realization of the rest. This theory of Eighteenth Century individualism, stated perhaps in unduly simplified form, does not in reality conflict with the theory of social order. The essence of the doctrine is that the claims and interests of human beings rest upon certain "natural rights." It does not follow, however, that such claims and interests may not receive support from other sources, and that those sources may not maintain a reciprocal relationship with natural rights. The case is indeed the opposite. Order is a necessary condition of human social life and it is impossible to imagine a society in which order of some sort does not exist. In so far as order is properly maintained all the demands and claims which are regarded as natural rights are protected; to the extent that it fails, they are in danger of being disregarded. For the achievement of their natural rights—life, business, property, family organization, etc.—men must therefore depend upon a state of order maintained through all the forms of social control. An adequate theory of natural rights will tell us what personal satisfactions deserve recognition and protection; a theory of social order will indicate the ways in which that end may be achieved.

THE MEANING OF ORDER

"In the Beginning was the Word." We need at the outset of a theory of social order a satisfactory working definition of order. It is a concept which is generally used in social thought without a fixed denotation, although the advantages of a precise vocabulary, particularly with respect to the basic words, have long been recognized. What do we mean by order? We say that a picture possesses order, that a room is disordered, that a soldier lives an ordered life. The man on the street would probably say that nature presented examples of order in the succession of day and night, the periodical rise and fall of the tide, the disappearance and return of planets and the other sequential phenomena that present themselves to his eyes. Let us look at a specific example, say, a room. It seems plain that when we say a room is orderly we mean that the objects in the room are related to one another in a certain way. The relationship in the present case may be either aesthetic or one of convenience. If either arrangement, or a combination of both, is desired we consider the characteristics of the various objects, and the characteristics which some of the objects possess fix their initial position, thereby determining wholly or in part the position of the other objects. That is to say, we are in the presence of order when we have a relationship among elements of the kind that when we know the characteristics of certain of the elements, the characteristics of the remaining elements are indicated. It is important to note that it is the *relation* which indicates the order and not the characteristics of the elements to be ordered.[2] The objects in a room can be arranged in a

[2] This is clearly brought out by Russell in his discussion of serial order in mathematics. "We must not look for the definition of order in the nature of the set of terms to be ordered, since one set of terms has many orders. The order lies, not in the *class* of terms, but in a relation among the members of the class, in respect of which some appear as earlier and some as later."—*Introduction to Mathematical Philosophy* (1930) 30. See also his *Principles of Mathematics* (1903) c. xxv, and Stebbing, *Modern Introduction to Logic* (1930) 228.

multitude of orderly ways, although their characteristics of course are constant. The relation, limiting it to one of aesthetics or convenience, determines the order by indicating the characteristics which are to be given prominence.

In society there are numerous systems of orders demanding many varieties of conduct on the part of the members. Our behavior must be conducted in accordance with the relations established by the Government, the church, the moral code of our community, the corner grocery at which we buy provisions, all the systems with which we come into contact. We are disorderly when we do not behave in the manner required by the relation. An attorney engaged in the trial of a case is an element in a court relation. That relation demands that his behavior, among other things, shall be respectful to the presiding judge; to the extent that it is disrespectful the attorney may be regarded as disorderly. What is disorderly from the point of view of a particular relation may be orderly from the standpoint of another. The conduct of a criminal is disorderly when viewed from the relationship existing between the citizen and the community; it may be entirely orderly, however, if we consider it from the narrower relationship which exists between the criminal and his own particular environment.

In the relatively few attempts which have been made by sociologists to explain the meaning of social order it has generally been conceived as the arrangement of human beings in a set of stable relationships. This conception is substantially accurate so far as it goes, but it overlooks the important point that we need to know what is meant by the term "relationship." It is the relationship which generates the order and which permits us, when we know the order which has been generated, to infer information, or to increase our knowledge, about matters not yet experienced. Not all relationships, however, permit an orderly arrangement or a basis for inference. Thus a relationship of color exists among three objects colored white, yellow and red respectively. On this basis alone, we are unable to determine what the orderly arrangement of the objects should be. If we desire order in such a case we have to utilize some other relationship such as size, or in the case of human beings, social status.

ORDER AND THE APPEARANCE OF LAW

Order so conceived is found in all known human societies. A society, or culture, it should be remembered, is something more than a fortuitous collection of elements; it represents a structure, a partly unified whole, in which the elements are inter-related and united so as to maintain that whole. That structure, although the number of elements entering into it, even in the case of the simplest peoples, is enormous, seems always to be erected in accordance with the same fundamental plan, or as Wissler terms it, "a universal culture pattern." [3] In this complex whole the behavior of human beings is ordered in accordance with the requirements of the relations established in the structure. No description of any society, primitive or civilized, has failed to disclose the existence of order in the behavior of its members. In all societies relations develop which determine or demand particular varieties of conduct on the part of its individuals. These relations are a universal and inescapable feature of the social order.

They are inescapable in the sense that in society men cannot act as if each were a Robinson Crusoe, a solitary individual following his own impulses and desires entirely without regard to the impulses and desires of other men. All human conduct is modified and influenced by relations. The

[3] *Man and Culture* (1923) 74. There is still, however, a lack of agreement with respect to the elements comprising the plan. For other conceptions of the pattern see Spencer, *Principles of Sociology* (1912); Morgan, *Ancient Society* (1871); Tylor, *Primitive Culture* (1889); Hankins, *Introduction to the Study of Society* (1928) 392; Folsom, *Culture and Social Progress* (1928) 22. For criticisms see Eubank, *Concepts of Sociology* (1932) 339; Ellwood, *Cultural Evolution* (1927) 95; Teggart, *Theory of History* (1925) 214.

behavior of an individual who pursues an isolated existence is ordered at the minimum by the recurrence of day and night and the seasons. The conduct of men living in a group will be ordered also by these relations and, in addition, by the relations established by the requirements of group life. In society men must make allowance, if only for their own well-being, for the desires of other men. Their relationship to other members of the group demands a particular type of conduct on their own part. Thus, as Ross [4] long ago recognized, order in society, though no doubt of a rough and imperfect kind, is an inevitable feature of group life even in the absence of intentional controls. Ross expressed the belief that sympathy, sociability, the sense of justice and resentment were competent by themselves to produce a natural social order without purposeful control. In this form, however, the theory depends upon an adequate individual and social psychology, something we are still without, and it appears sounder to base it upon the recognition of the inevitable appearance in group life of relations which order the behavior of the members.

Thus order originates in a relation. But the relation and the particular type of conduct which it demands are, in the absence of purposeful control, seldom, if ever, perceived as such. Primitive man could be aware of them as such only by the processes of rational thought and there is no evidence that problems of this type ever entered his head. Two ways only are open for the discovery of the behavior required by a relation: trial and reflective thought. We may be sure that it was the method of trial which, in all but an infinitesimal number of cases, led to the specific orderly conduct needed to satisfy the relation. Here also there was of course, except in the rarest instances, no perception of a possibility of an alternative course of action and a calculated choice of one. There was only a necessity to act, action, and then the result. If the result did not satisfy the relation a different form of behavior was followed when the necessity again arose. This appears to

4 *Social Control* (1901) 41.

be the general pattern, prior to or in the absence of purposeful control, which accounts for the development of the particular type of conduct demanded by a specific relation.
Whether or not the consequences of definite orderly conduct
satisfy the relation must always of course be judged from the
position of the special society in which it occurs. We are able
to perceive that the principle of totemism contains some elements of harm. It forbids the eating of certain foods which are
sometimes abundant in the locality and thus decreases the
available food supply. But from the standpoint of the people
practising totemism the consequences of conduct which observes that principle outweigh in desirability the consequences
of a lessened food supply.

When orderly behavior has once been established and
stabilized we apply to such behavior the general term *custom*.
But custom is also something more than an established mode
of activity. It is a rule of conduct, one of the means of social
control.[5] It is important to have this distinction before us
when we consider the process by which behavior becomes
customary in the sense that it is orderly. The classic explanation of this process, borrowed from Nineteenth Century psychology, is that orderly behavior is a habit, and that it has
become a habit essentially through repetition. In the interests
of generality, however, it is advisable to study the persistence
of orderly behavior, in the absence of purposeful control, under the wider term "learning." An established mode of activity
has been learned. By what process has this occurred? Repetition, although it may be a factor in numerous cases, is not
sufficient to explain all cases of learning. As we know from
modern psychology learning often occurs, in the case of individuals, without repetition, as the result of a single performance.[6] In order to determine how a mode of activity becomes established without the aid of conscious controls we

---

[5] 1 Westermarck, *Origin and Development of the Moral Ideas* (2nd
ed., 1912) 118; Ross, *Social Control* (1904) 184.

[6] Dunlap, *Habits* (1932) 77 *et seq.*

must look at the occasion when the action first occurs. If the results of the activity, whether consciously perceived or not, are of a kind which will be sought again in the future, the same activity will be repeated. The orderly behavior may be learned as a result of one performance or it may take many performances to stabilize it. In any event, whatever may be the necessary factors in individual learning, the essential factor in social learning is the "result"; that is the factor which determines whether the action shall be repeated. If the process of repetition is once initiated it may, and often does, continue to a point at which the original "consequence" is altogether forgotten. It is a commonplace of sociological knowledge that the inertia of custom is a feature of both primitive and civilized societies. During the initiation period among the Australian Kroatun certain food was prohibited. A young native was asked, "But if you were hungry and caught a female opossum, you might eat it if the old men were not there." The boy replied, "I could not do that; it would not be right"; and he could give no other reason except that he could not disregard the customs, i.e., the rules, of his people.[7] It is the invariable response; no reply other than "This is the way it is done" occurs, or can be given, by a native in most of the cases in which he is questioned about his habits. Any other answer would in fact appear to him eccentric.

The theory of the rise of custom here put forward is based upon inference and it would seem impossible to illustrate it in practice. Nevertheless a theory of the development of custom in its generality is necessary as a foundation for an adequate social theory of law. Theories of the possible origins of custom illuminate and emphasize the social basis of the legal order. They show us the predominating elements of irrationality and complexity in the legal process; they reveal the unlikely circumstance that a single basic factor operates exclusively as the controlling element in the functioning of the social system.

[7] Fison and Howitt, *Kaunlaroi and Kurnai* (1880) 256 *et seq.*

Anthropological thought has devised methods for handling the question of the origin of specific customs. Inference, however, still remains, and possibly will always remain, the only method available for the determination of the origin of custom generally. The theories of diffusion, independent origin, convergence and its corollary, the principle of limitation of possibilities, are available for inquiries into the origin of specific customs. These methods have been tested in countless cases, and while they are still remote from any finality, they represent a vast advance over the prior essentially haphazard methods. But the origins of custom, the family, language and a host of other biological and social products are lost in mystery. "We go up the stream of history," Sumner [8] wrote, "to the utmost point for which we have evidence of its course. Then we are forced to reach out into the darkness upon the line of direction marked by the remotest course of the historic stream." Mankind possesses an insatiable thirst for knowledge of the origin of things and, provided we recognize the limitations of that knowledge, efforts to satisfy the thirst have tangible value.

In the world of order, law appears as one of the instruments which stabilize and modify modes of activity. It is one of the means of social control. In sociological literature the term "social control" has been used with a variety of meanings, dependent upon whether the source or the purpose of control was stressed. In its widest and most useful sense, however, it includes every way through which human society exercises a modifying influence upon itself or any part of itself.[9] Law is that means of social control regulating human conduct which, for its enforcement, embodies in itself, or has behind it, a definite agency which exerts, or through which may be exerted, the pressure of politically organized society. We must beware, Thurnwald has warned us, of assuming a supercilious egocentric position. Law in the forms

[8] Sumner, *Folkways* (1906) 7.
[9] *Cf.* Eubank, *Concepts of Sociology* (1932) 220.

we know it in the Western World is, as he remarked of the modern state, no more than several of many abstract possibilities. We must be prepared, upon the basis of the principle of equivalents, to recognize as law many social forms to which, if they obtain in our own society, the term could not properly be applied. In other words, we must not assume, as Durkheim [10] did in his study of the Australian totem system, that a painstaking study of the law of one people will reveal the essential elements of law in its generality. We are entitled to assume universally only that which we have in fact or in sound theory good reason to believe may be put universally.

Sociologists studying law as an instrument of social control have thought of that aspect of the legal order which Mr. Justice Cardozo has aptly termed the judicial process. They think about the machinery of law, its instruments of compulsion, what officials do about disputes and about the rules of law. It is in this sense that Ross examined law in his now classic work *Social Control.* From this position the judicial process is the "law" which is the means of social control. The set of rules of conduct which the English analytical jurists assumed was "law" is, in this theory, merely a formulation or abstract scheme of the legal order which obtains or results from the functioning of the judicial process. It is not the "law" but a series of shorthand descriptions of the legal order which, when taken in their total, describe the legal order in its entirety. Malinowski's [11] much discussed conception of law in the Trobriands as a body of binding obligations, thought of as rightful claim on one side and as duty on the other, "kept in force by a specific mechanism of reciprocity and publicity inherent in the structure of their society" is included within this theory. In the Trobriands the principle of reciprocity is the "law"; it is the instrument of compulsion, the equivalent of the judicial process in Western society. The so-called body

[10] *Les Formes élémentaires de la vie religieuse* (1912) 593.

[11] *Crime and Custom in Savage Society* (1926) 58; *idem,* Introduction to Hogbin, *Law and Order in Polynesia* (1934).

of binding obligations is the anthropologists' description of the legal order which results from the operation of the principle of reciprocity. But this is plainly a one-sided view of the facts. Law as a means of social control includes much more than merely the judicial process. It includes all aspects of the legal order which do in fact influence social behavior. One of these aspects, obviously, is the set of legal rules. They are imperatives or norms, ordering or indicating what men shall do, and, as such, exercise a modifying effect on human behavior. They may be, and frequently are, obeyed entirely apart from any thought of the judicial process or compulsion. In this respect they are on a plane with rules of custom, which, as Cicero [12] pointed out, are precepts in themselves. They are distinguished from customary rules only in the respect that behind them lies a specific agency of political society for their enforcement. It must be granted also that the idealistic elements in law, our notions of what is just or natural, which the philosophical jurists since at least the days of Plato have endlessly debated, are embraced within the concept of law as an instrument of order. From time to time they assume the form of legal precepts and also directly influence judicial decision. A familiar example in our own system is the ideals which have found expression in the decisions of the United States Supreme Court construing the phrase "due process of law," which, by its very wording and absence of content directs judicial inquiry to conceptions of justice and right.

It is perhaps unnecessary, though no doubt safer, to add that the primary purpose of the definition of law here put forward is to distinguish it, as an instrument of control, from the other instruments of control such as custom, propaganda and public opinion. Clear thinking demands that we know as precisely as possible what it is we are to discuss; it is one of the chief weaknesses of Ehrlich,[13] who, like Aristotle,

[12] *De Officiis,* i. 41.
[13] *Sociology of Law* (1936) 24, 169.

Aquinas and Kant, sees law in terms of order, that he nowhere makes clear what he means by law or how it is to be distinguished from other orderings. There is no thought, in the definition here suggested, that an essential element of the law is that its rules are obeyed because of its compulsive aspect. Legal precepts in fact, in our society at any rate, are, more often than not, obeyed without the idea of compulsion ever entering men's minds. Compulsion, moreover, in this sense raises an entirely different question than the one we are now considering. We are here attempting a classification; compulsion is one aspect of the entirely different problem, Why is law obeyed? One other point with respect to the definition should be emphasized. The use of the term "political" is not meant to imply that law is determined exclusively by political factors, a view entertained by some jurists. Many factors—political, economic, ethical, psychologic, etc.— influence the legal order and none of them is exclusive. The use of the term "political" is meant only to indicate to which aspect of society the enforcement agency is to be assigned. The allotment to the political assists in the distinction. It rules out, for example, religious precepts supported by the force of that part of society.

THE THEORY OF STAGES

Maine, Post, McLennan and the other Nineteenth Century jurists who, under the influence of Darwinism, attempted to describe general trends of social and legal development were attempting a task of the first importance. They were engaged in the pursuit of one of the ideals of science, namely, the formulation of abstract universal laws.

The realization of that task is still before us, but we know today that we must look in other directions for its accomplishment. Undoubtedly the most famous generalization achieved by the evolutionary jurists was Maine's [14] theory of legal history as a movement from status to contract. Histori-

[14] *Ancient Law*, c. 5 (1861).

cally, however, as many writers have shown, the generalization is at most only partly true. Moreover, it lacks the elements of universality and certainty which are necessary concomitants of scientific laws. Maine himself recognized the unsoundness of the general theory of stages of development which prevailed at the time. "There has been room," he [15] wrote, "for many courses of modification and development, each proceeding within its own area. So far as I am aware there is nothing in the recorded history of society to justify the belief that, during the vast chapter of its growth which is wholly unwritten, the same transformations of social constitution succeeded one another everywhere, uniformly if not simultaneously." Few, if any, today hold the belief that there have been regular sequences in the development of the elements of culture which always recur in the same order. This belief, however, was at one time widely held and, in juristic circles, was adopted particularly by Post [16] who claimed, for example, that "monogamous marriage originally emerged everywhere from pure communism in women, through the intermediate stages of limited communism in women, polyandry, and polygyny." Such beliefs, however, represented merely the first unthoughtful attempts to apply the evolutionary methods in social thought.

This method was soon supplanted by the attempt to describe general trends of social development rather than to isolate and work out a detailed history of particular elements. A long list of notable names—Comte, Hegel, Marx, Westermarck, Sumner, Hobhouse—is associated with this enterprise. The schemes of development put forward in accordance with this method have also been subject to extensive criticism, but as Ginsberg [17] has recently pointed out they suggest a theory of the causes underlying the historical process, of

[15] *Dissertations on Early Law and Custom* (1883) 218.
[16] *Die Geschlechtsgenossenschaft der Urzeit und die Entstehung der Ehe* (1875) 17.
[17] *Studies in Sociology* (1932) 88.

which they show a much richer insight than do the previous schemes. He concludes that the conception of stages of growth is still necessary and useful, and that it may be defended against the objections which have been raised against it.

Elaborate schemes, supported by an extensive mass of material, have been worked out by Westermarck, Hobhouse and Sumner [18] to illustrate the stages in the formation of societary control. These stages have been summarized by Eubank [19] as follows:

1. An *emotion* of approval or disapproval in a *particular* case.

2. A *judgment* of approval or disapproval constituting a generalization as to the desirability of cases of this *type*.

3. *Folkways, Mores, and Usages*, informal non-institutionalized embodiments of previously formed judgments of approval or disapproval, but generally understood and commonly accepted as applying to all cases of this *general class*.

4. Accepted *institutions*, culminating in *law*, the formal crystallization of the previously formed judgments of approval or disapproval, into *express statutes*, with definite penalties for violation.

It should be emphasized again that the scheme of development here summarized is not put forward as historically true in the sense that the stages are repeated in the same order with respect to each form of conduct which is the subject of control. It is obvious that if society has once learned the value of express statutory control it is entirely feasible for it to pass over the stage represented by folkways. We have no direct evidence that in any society the scheme is historically true as a first attempt. What evidence we do possess indicates indeed the contrary. Furthermore, there is considerable doubt

[18] Westermarck, *Origin and Development of the Moral Ideas* (1912); Hobhouse, *Morals and Evolution* (1915); Sumner, *Folkways* (1906).

[19] *Op. cit., supra* note 9 at 248.

whether emotional approval or disapproval is properly regarded as the primary source of social control. Breach of custom or habit seems to be the source of sympathetic resentment, which does not appear to be a distinctive inner feeling giving rise to acts.[20] Its chief value lies in the fact that it appears to describe a general trend, and as such it may throw some illumination upon the process of legal development. It can never be, however, the basis of a sound general theory of law. It lacks the first requirement of such a theory—generality. No doubt the theory puts its finger upon something significant in legal development but it falls far short of including within its scope the whole of the legal process.

[20] Dewey, *Human Nature and Conduct* (1930) 76.

3.

THE FORMATION OF LAW

WE HAVE SEEN THAT ORDER, as here conceived, is found in all known human societies. We have seen also that order originates in a relation, and that the particular type of orderly conduct demanded by a specific relation, prior to or in the absence of purposeful control, is the product in general of the method of invention and trial. These observations, however, serve only to introduce us to the general problem of the formation of the legal order. They fall far short of completeness when we examine the development of the legal order in any of the societies of which we have knowledge.

At this point it is necessary to understand what is meant by culture, the nature of its formation and its relationship to law. Culture is the core of any general theory of society and hence of law; it is the essential subject matter of social thought.

One of the chief products of the association of human beings is what anthropologists, sociologists and others term culture. It may be defined as the composite of products which results from human association. As such it includes, among many other things, material goods, knowledge and beliefs, art, institutions, custom and law. It is important to note that culture results only from association of human beings in groups, and that it is always an invention of man. Culture is a social product, the result of the activities and thought of human beings in association. It is doubtful if a group consisting of a few individuals only could develop a culture except of the most rudimentary kind. At bottom, culture, while it is the direct product of human association, is in one of its ultimate factors the result of the workings of the human mind, and the human mind is essentially a social product. "It is not so much the result of structural and physiological characters," Briffault[1] points out, "as of the characters of social groups, of their constitution, of the relations between their component individuals." Conceptual thought, which is the essential feature of the human mind, in turn depends upon language, and language itself cannot develop in the isolated individual or in small groups. Culture is also an invention of man in the quite obvious sense that it is not a creation of nature. It is nature modified by human labor and by human thought.

Three principal elements operate in the formation of the culture of any society: (a) invention, (b) communication and (c) what is termed, more or less improperly,[2] social heredity. The rules relating to succession to property afford probably the most satisfactory illustration of the operation of these three basic processes. Certain culture traits, such as exogamy, cooking, fire-making, and the use of twisted string, are known to be universal among present-day societies. It is scarcely necessary to turn to anthropological data, of which

[1] *Evolution of Human Species* (1927) 41 Scientia 403.

[2] Warden, *The Emergence of Human Culture* (1936) 20, states "the term 'social heredity' is a vicious misnomer as applied to the workings of culture. The transmission of culture from generation to generation is secured by the process of group conditioning." His theory, however, fails to take account of the direct passing on from one generation to another of the ideas of the preceding generation, as distinguished from its habits of thought and action which may be the result of the process of group conditioning. The term "social heredity" is in such general use, with a more or less fixed content, that its continued employment appears desirable.

there is an abundance, to demonstrate the universality of the inheritance of property. The members of all present-day societies possess property of some sort [3] and upon the death of a member the society is faced with the problem of disposing of his effects. There are a limited number of things that can happen to a man's property after his death. His property, as in a number of communities, can be entirely destroyed; it can be appropriated by the community or individual members thereof; it can be distributed to certain designated people in accordance with fixed rules; his family, or group, or particular members of it may be permitted in their own discretion to determine how his property shall be distributed, or finally, the owner of the property may himself, with or without conditions, be permitted to say how the property, or parts of it, shall be distributed, and his wishes will be carried out. In the attempts of the various societies to meet these limited possibilities we can observe the practical operation of the three basic mechanisms, invention, communication and social heredity, in the formation of culture and its particular aspect we are here studying, law.

INVENTION

It is customary to distinguish between invention and discovery; the former may be defined as the creation by man of new forms or processes and the latter as the perception of forms or processes already existent but unrecognized.[4] Although there is a sharp distinction between the two processes they are in fact closely inter-related. Moreover, using the general term "invention" to cover both processes, it is obvious

[3] Beaglehole, *Property* (1931) *passim;* Lowie, *Primitive Society* (1920) 205; 2 Westermarck, *Origin and Development of the Moral Ideas* (1917) 1.

[4] Dixon, *The Building of Cultures* (1928) 35 makes the point of difference turn on *purpose,* which he assigns to invention; but as Eubank, *The Concepts of Sociology* (1932) 361 correctly points out, both discovery and invention may be either accidental or purposeful.

that all new culture traits must be the product of this process. Thus, if we had sufficient knowledge to permit us to trace culture traits to their source we would find that all were the result of invention. The last will and testament is an instance of the inventive process. Modern English legal historians have attempted to explain its appearance by the existence of an avaricious priestly class and a grasping Church.

Maine long ago expressed a doubt whether the will would ever have come into being at all if it had not been for the remarkable ideas of the Romans with respect to universal succession. "To the Romans," he [5] wrote, "belongs preëminently the credit of inventing the will." He also believed that it was "doubtful whether a true power of testation was known to any original society except the Romans." [6] But it was the Church, he pointed out, which had much to do with the rapid assimilation of the Imperial conception of the will by the barbarians. The religious foundations owed their temporal possessions almost exclusively to private bequests, and thus the decrees of the earliest Provincial Councils frequently contain anathemas against those who deny the sanctity of wills. In England, he believed, the Church was certainly chief among the causes which led to the adoption from the Romans of the notion of the will. Maitland's subtle imagination seized upon this concept, and with characteristic ingenuity carried it a step forward. Priestly exhortations were responsible, he [7] declared, for the origin of the practice of testamentary dispositions. The only necessary supposition is to imagine an age when testamentary dispositions are unknown and land is rarely sold or given away. A law of intestate succession in such a time will take deep root in men's thoughts and habits. But in the course of time wealth becomes amassed and purchasers desire to acquire the land; in addition there are bishops and

[5] Maine, *Ancient Law* (World's Classics ed. 1931) 161.
[6] *Id.* at 163.
[7] 2 Pollock and Maitland, *History of English Law* (2nd ed. 1899) 249 and 314 *et seq.*

priests desirous of acquiring the land by gift and willing to offer spiritual benefits in return. At this point a struggle begins and the law must decide whether the claims of expectant heirs can be defeated. There will be a compromise, a series of compromises and then there will be recognition of testamentary dispositions. This explanation of the origin of the testament has appeared at least plausible to Holdsworth,[8] who has adopted it in its entirety.

But the will is not indigenous to European civilization. Among other peoples we find it assuming other forms and serving other purposes. In certain cultures power of testamentary disposition is allowed in order to prevent disputes. Thus, among the natives of Borneo, at a man's death his property is divided between his widow and her children. But the division of the inheritance frequently leads to disputes, and an old man before his death is permitted to indicate the manner in which his property shall be divided.[9] The same rule prevails among certain of the Melanesians, at least with respect to the inheritance of canoes.[10] Instances are also found where certain kinds of property descend by operation of law, while other property may be willed. Among the Southern Massim a man may, when ill, express a desire that particular articles of jewelry descend to his children and his wishes will be respected.[11] Land, among the Louisiades, descends by operation of law to members of the clan, but a man may leave his personal property in part to his children by telling his clansmen, on whom such property would devolve, that he wishes such and such a piece of property to pass to a particular child.[12] A man belongs to his mother's clan, not his father's, among the Crows of the Western Plains, and his property descends

[8] 2 Holdsworth, *History of English Law* (3d ed. 1923) 91 *et seq.*

[9] 1 Hose and McDougall, *The Pagan Tribes of Borneo* (1912) 83.

[10] Codrington, *The Melanesians* (1891) 63.

[11] Seligmann, *The Melanesians of British New Guinea* (1910) 423 *et seq.*

[12] *Id.* at 739.

to his brothers and sisters or, if none survive, to other members of his own clan. But on his deathbed he may bequeath a few articles to his wife or son; otherwise they would receive nothing.[13] An Aztec by a deathbed disposition was permitted to disinherit a senior heir in favor of a junior.[14] When a Samoan feels that he is about to die he will apportion part of his estate and his wishes will generally be respected. But the bulk of his property is left to be divided according to native custom.[15]

Instances of true power of testamentary disposition are also found among primitive peoples. The practice of *tutuing*, or devising by will, was found to exist among the natives of Tahiti prior to the arrival of the first missionaries.[16] It was employed with respect to all classes of property, including land. They could not, of course, leave a written will, as they possessed no written language; but during a season of illness, members of the family or confidential friends were called together; and the ill man gave directions for the disposal of his effects after his decease. The directions were considered a sacred charge, and were usually executed with fidelity. Similarly, among the Akikuyu of British East Africa, a man on his deathbed calls for his family and the old men, and in their presence makes a final division of his goods. Theoretically, he has absolute power of appointment, but in practice, however, his bequests are largely dictated by custom.[17] If a Uhamba feels that he is nearing his end he will assemble his sons, and to the eldest he will probably say, "The goats belonging to such a hut shall be yours." He will then call another son and say, "The goats of such and such a hut shall be yours, and if any of you break these wishes he will surely die." He will then mention a certain *shamba* (cultivated field) and say,

[13] Murdock, *Our Primitive Contemporaries* (1934) 272.
[14] *Id.* at 372.
[15] Brown, *Melanesians and Polynesians* (1910) 288, 384.
[16] 2 Ellis, *Polynesian Researches* (1830) 361.
[17] Routledge, *With a Prehistoric People* (1910) 143.

"Such and such a *shamba* shall not be sold and if this wish is broken the one who sells it shall die." This operates as an entail on the property, and, such is the strength of the injunction it will be passed on from generation to generation.[18] A New Zealander who has acquired land by purchase or conquest may will it to whomsoever he choose.[19] A native of the Savage Island possesses testamentary power with respect to all property except such as must be destroyed out of respect to his memory.[20] True testamentary powers also obtain among the natives of the Torres Straits,[21] and Bangala [22] of the Upper Congo River, and the Veddas.[23] Among the two latter peoples, an effort to overcome the difficulties met with because of the absence of written wills is observable. In the Bangala culture, when property is left by will, a token is given to the beneficiary in the presence of witnesses and the article or articles named. The eldest son is then informed of the token, the person to whom it was given and the nature of the goods bequeathed. After the testator's death the token is taken to the eldest son and the property handed over in the presence of witnesses. A similar practice obtains among the Veddas.

We are, with respect to the problem of the origin of the testament, presented with the necessity of choosing between diffusion and independent origin or invention. The evidence available in this case points to independent invention, and, more specifically, to the particular process known as con-

[18] Hobley, *Further Researches into Kikuyu and Kamba Religious Beliefs and Customs* (1911) 41 Journal of the Royal Anthropological Institute 406, 427.

[19] 2 Polack, *Manners and Customs of the New Zealanders* (1840) 69; *cf.* Shortland, *Traditions and Superstitions of the New Zealanders* (1856) 271.

[20] Thomson, *Note upon the Natives of Savage Island, or Niué* (1901) 31 Journal of the Royal Anthropological Institute 137, 143.

[21] 5 *Reports of the Cambridge Anthropological Expedition to Torres Straits* (1904) 285-87.

[22] Weeks, *Anthropological Notes on the Bangala of the Upper Congo River* (1909) 39 Journal of the Royal Anthropological Institute 416, 426.

[23] Seligmann, *The Veddas* (1911) 115.

vergence. The doctrine of convergence in anthropology is used to explain similarities of culture traits arising from dissimilar sources, or similar artifacts arising independently in unconnected areas. It is a term borrowed from biology, paleontology, botany and other natural sciences, where it has approximately the same meaning. Goldenweiser [24] has shown that a limitation of possibilities invites convergence. If there is a desire to do a certain thing there is frequently a limited number of ways in which the end can be accomplished. Oars can differ in an infinite variety of ways; but a *good* oar will of necessity have certain characteristics. It must not be too long or too short, too heavy or too light, too brittle or too pliable, it must be flat, and also slightly curved longitudinally and laterally; the butt end must be adjusted to manipulation; finally, the oar should be of a material which will float, so that it can readily be recovered from the water. No one will believe that the oar has been invented only once in history. It would also be absurd to assume that the precise stages, initial and subsequent, in the development of oars in different localities were identical or even markedly similar. But ultimately, one way or another, there emerges a good oar with certain relatively fixed features determined by conditions of effective use. Thus the histories of the oar in different places, Goldenweiser points out, represent a set of convergent processes.

This process would also appear to explain the invention of the testament in unconnected areas. The practice of testamentary disposition has occurred too infrequently, and in unconnected culture areas, for it to be attributed to diffusion generally. To some extent borrowing has undoubtedly taken place, particularly in the Western culture area, but it would be too fanciful to explain the practice among the Tahitians on the same ground. As we have seen above, there are a limited number of things that can happen to a man's property after his death. Sooner or later, for the same or different rea-

[24] Goldenweiser, *History, Psychology and Culture* (1933) 45 *et seq.*

sons, the probabilities are such that several communities, for a definite period at least, will utilize one of the methods described above. There is thus an instance of convergence in the fact that the practice of testation is found in the Western culture area and in Melanesia. Testation, it need scarcely be added, is not the only such instance in the field of inheritance. Another example is the English rule of heriot, which also obtains in Melanesia.[25]

COMMUNICATION

Primogeniture is a convenient example of the second process, borrowing or diffusion. Certain aspects of this process are well known to legal students under the name of Reception, a title applied by German scholars to the diffusion of Roman law in Western Europe during the Middle Ages and afterwards. In fact, the concept of diffusion was developed in legal theory long prior to its appearance in modern anthropological thought. It may be fairly observed that no study of the process of diffusion put forward by anthropologists yet equals the classic works of legal students on the reception of Roman law in their wealth of detail and in their comprehensive analysis of the social forces connected with the process.

Blackstone [26] found two reasons for the existence of primogeniture. He believed that it was connected with the rule which required titles of nobility to descend to the eldest son alone. This example, he held, was further enforced by the inconveniences that attended the splitting up of estates; "namely, the division of military services, the multitude of infant tenants incapable of performing any duty, the consequential weakening of the strength of the kingdom, and the inducing younger sons to take up with the business and idleness of a country life, instead of being serviceable to themselves and the public, by engaging in mercantile, in military, in civil, or in ecclesiastical employment." One need scarcely

[25] Rivers, *Social Organization* (1924) 116.
[26] 2 Bl. Comm. *215.

be told that these words were written in the Eighteenth Century. They exhibit the fundamental weakness of much of the social thought of that period. Hard problems were solved by the swift processes of argument, and the assumptions were taken for granted with the self-satisfaction which the Romantics and the Victorians were later to find so intolerable. If Eighteenth Century thinkers failed to realize that the validity of their arguments depended upon the truth of their premises, later generations did not. "It seems to be thought," Maitland [27] wrote in a notable paragraph in 1879, "that a vague reference to 'feudalism' is a sufficient account of the origin of primogeniture. Perhaps familiarity with this law has blunted our power of discrimination. We are so accustomed to see all the ages jumbled together in our Nineteenth Century law that nothing surprises us, and any semblance of explanation which may be offered for existing institutions is accepted as satisfactory. 'Feudalism' is a good word, and will cover a multitude of ignorances. To ask what was the real connection between feudalism and primogeniture would argue a reprehensible discontent with beliefs sanctioned by Blackstone and orthodoxy." Maitland [28] himself felt that the rule of primogeniture was not a natural part of the law of inheritance, in the sense that, if the dictates of justice alone were followed, land would be divided equally among the heirs. He therefore concluded that when the law of inheritance decides that the whole land shall go to one son it is not thinking merely of what would be fair with respect to the dead man and his sons, but "it has in view one who is a stranger to the inheritance, some king or some lord, whose interests demand that the land shall not be partitioned." This assumption led Maitland to the conclusion that the rule of primogeniture, which was in England apparently first applied to military fiefs, came into existence to protect the interest of the lord. In this way it was simpler for the lord to get his services. Similarly, the same principle requires that

---

[27] Maitland, 1 *Collected Papers* (1911) 175.
[28] 2 Pollock and Maitland, *op. cit. supra* note 7, at 262-274.

the rights of the unfree peasant in a tenement shall descend to one person. The lord looks to the eldest for the due performance of the services, and the claims of the younger brothers become merely moral, not enforced by the king's court. This is now, in the legal field, the generally accepted explanation of the rule of primogeniture. It has been adopted by Holdsworth [29] without reservation.

The scholarly and conscientious industry with which the historians of English law have sought the origins of primogeniture in remote English customs cannot fail to command our admiration. The student of a custom in its generality must be grateful, as Westermarck [30] has observed, to the specialist who provides him with the results of his detailed research, but a wider view often helps the specialist to explain facts which he could hardly understand in full if his knowledge is restricted to a limited area. If we adopt this position we are confronted immediately with the fact that primogeniture is not peculiar to English law and the systems, in the United States and elsewhere, derived from it. It is not a rule found exclusively even in the so-called advanced cultures. In many societies the eldest son [31] is the chief or only heir; or, where

[29] 3 Holdsworth, *op. cit. supra* note 8, at 172.

[30] 1 Westermarck, *History of Human Marriage* (5th ed. 1922) 17.

[31] Walckenaer, 15 *Collection des relations de voyages* (1842) 380; Tuhnberg, *An Account of the Cape of Good Hope* in 16 Pinkerton, *Voyages and Travels in all Parts of the World* (1814) 142 (Hottentots); M'Lennan, *Primitive Marriage* (1865) 188 (Nair); 2 Johnston, *The Uganda Protectorate* (1902) 828; 1 Post, *Grundriss der ethnologischen Jurisprudence* (1894) 217, 221 (Organ-Ulu, Komering-Ulu, Nias); 2 Polack, *op. cit. supra* note 19, at 69; 2 Junghuhn, *Die Battalander auf Sumatra* (1847) 147; Erckert, *Der Kaukasus und seine Völker* (1887) 115 (Ossetes); Kohler, *Ueber die Gewohnheitsrechte von Bengalen* (1890) 9; Zeitschr. f. vergleichende Rechtswiss, 321, 336 (Kumis); Kohler, *Indische Gewohnheitsrechte* (1889) 8 *id.* 89, 131 (Deccan); Jenks, *The Bontoc Igorot* (1905) 165; Jennes and Ballentyne, *The Northern D'Entrecasteaux* (1920) 72; Barton, *Notes on the Suk Tribe of the Kenia Colony* (1921) 51 Journal of the Royal Anthropological Institute 99; Dalton, *Descriptive Ethnology of Bengal* (1872) 13 (Singhpos);

the maternal system of descent is in operation, the eldest uterine brother,[32] or the eldest son of the eldest uterine sister,[33] inherits. Sometimes, however, the inheritance by the eldest son of all or a major share of the property of his father carries with it the duty to support the remaining members of

---

Chanler, *Through Jungle and Desert* (1896) 316 (Rendile); Bosman, *A New and Accurate Description of the Gold Coast* (1705) 203; Hinde, *The Last of the Masai* (1901) 51; Kingsley, *Travels in West Africa* (1897) 485 ("some tribes"); Gill, *Life in the Southern Isles* (1876) 46 (Maoris); 1 Crantz, *History of Greenland* (1820) 176; Risley, *Census of India,* 1901; Ethnographic Appendices (1903) 183, 203 (Bagdis, Limbus); Paulitschke, *Ethnographie Nordost Afrikas* (1893) 192 (Gallas); Muntzinger, *Sitten und Recht der Gogos* (1859) 69; Anon., *Inheritance and "Patria Potesta" in China,* 5 The China Rev. (1877) 404, 406; 2 Mariner, *The Natives of the Tonga Islands* (1817) 97, *cf.* 89 *et seq.;* Hollis, *The Nandi* (1909) 73; Chalmers, *Pioneering in New Guinea* (1887) 188; Weeks, *Among Congo Cannibals* (1913) 111; Hagen, *Die Bana* (1912) 2 Baessler-Archiv. 103; Dundas, *The Organization and Laws of Some Bantu Tribes in East Africa* (1915) 45 Journal of the Royal Anthropological Institute 294; MacDonald, *Manners, Customs, Superstitions and Religions of South African Tribes* (1890) 19 Journal of the Royal Anthropological Institute 277; Teit, *The Thompson River Indians of British Columbia* (1900); 2 Memoirs of the American Museum of Natural History 294.

[32] Proyart, *History of Loango, Kagongo,* in 16 Pinkerton, *Voyages and Travels in all Parts of the World* (1814) 571. The eldest uterine brother, if there is one, inherits. In the absence of brothers, the property goes to the eldest son of the eldest uterine sister, or lastly to the eldest son of the nearest maternal relation. Ellis, *The Tshi-Speaking Peoples* (1887) 298. *Cf.* Bosman, *op. cit., supra* note 31, at 203. Bosman ventured the following explanation of this particular custom: "I am of the opinion that this custom was introduced on account of the whoredom of the women, therein following the Custom of some *East-Indian* Kings, who (as Authors say) educate their sisters Son as their own, and appoint him to succeed on the throne, because they are more sure that their sisters Son is of their blood than they can be of their own." *Ibid.*

[33] Kingsley, *op. cit. supra* note 31, at 374; Torday and Joyce, *Notes on the Ethnography of the Ba-Yaka* (1906) 36 Journal of the Royal Anthropological Institute 44; *Ibid., Notes on the Ethnography of the Ba-Mbala* (1905) 35 Journal of the Royal Anthropological Institute 411. *Cf.* 2 Westermarck, *op. cit. supra* note 3, at 46.

the family. Thus, among the natives of Uganda Protectorate,[34] the eldest son inherits all the property but he must support his mother, stepmothers, brothers and sisters. Among the Rendile [35] "primogeniture is in vogue, but it is customary for the younger brothers to receive substantial presents. The heir assumes the care of his mother and sisters. In return for the care he bestows upon his sisters, all goods paid for them upon marriage go to him." The eldest son always inherits among some of the principal peoples of Siberia, but he is bound to make a certain provision for the younger son, even though his younger brother should be richer than himself.[36] Among the Masai [37] "the eldest male child inherits everything but it devolves upon him to look after and support the dead man's wives and all the other children. He practically assumes the position of father, though he may waive his responsibilities by parting with some of his inheritance to his relatives." Substantially the same rule applies in other localities.[38]

Various explanations of the rule of primogeniture have been suggested by ethnologists of the older school. Mary Kingsley [39] and Westermarck [40] believe that the underlying idea is the desire to keep the wealth of the house together, and if it were allowed to pass into the hands of weak people, like women and young children, this would not be done. Frazer [41] suggests that, in some instances at least, when there has been a change of social conditions, ultimogeniture, or the right of the youngest son to the exclusive inheritance, tends to pass into primogeniture. The fact that the first born son is regarded as a sacred being is sometimes held as the cause of primogeni-

[34] Johnston, *loc. cit. supra* note 31.

[35] Chanler, *loc. cit. supra* note 31.

[36] 1 Frazer, *Folk-Lore in the Old Testament* (1918) 476.

[37] Hinde, *loc. cit. supra* note 31.

[38] Munzinger, *op. cit. supra* note 31, at 74; Crantz, *loc. cit. supra* note 31.

[39] Kingsley, *loc. cit. supra* note 31.

[40] 2 Westermarck, *op. cit. supra* note 3, at 55.

[41] 2 Frazer, *op. cit. supra* note 36, at 484.

ture.[42] Risley[43] finds the origin of the rule in the duty of the eldest son who inherits an extra share of the property to support the other members of the family. The extra share "seems to be intended to enable him to support the female members of the family, who remain under his care." Maine [44] took the position that primogeniture could be traced to the succession of the eldest son to the headship of the tribe, which embodied the continuity of the chieftain's power. Miller [45] has similarly attempted to work out an evolutionary development. He thinks that the exigencies of life inevitably produce a set of conditions under which one of the children must assume the office of direct heir to the deceased. At first, the son who is chosen is not necessarily the oldest one but one who may have distinguished himself more than the other brothers. In Sumatra an eldest son was asked why he was passed over in favor of a younger brother. He answered with great naïveté: "Because I am accounted weak and silly." At this stage a system of primogeniture has not yet been evolved; inheritance by the eldest son is still dependent upon the possession of favorable personal qualities that fit him for these responsibilities. Miller believes, however, that the accumulating force of many individual instances soon serves to create a customary usualness which amounts to a folkway, namely, favoring the eldest son with a larger share of the inheritance. Experience attests to the beneficial nature of this usage and it then becomes "just" and "right" and even "moral" that the eldest son carry off the largest portion of the father's effects.

That the rule of primogeniture came into English law as a result of diffusion there can be little doubt. It was not, as Cecil [46] points out, "a plant of indigenous growth." It appears

[42] Gill, *op. cit. supra* note 31, at 46-47.
[43] Risley, *op. cit. supra* note 31, at 183.
[44] Maine, *Early History of Institutions* (1875) 198; *Ancient Law* 193 *et seq.*
[45] Miller, *The Child in Primitive Society* (1928) 231-232.
[46] Cecil, *Primogeniture* (1895) 26.

to have migrated to England as an appendage to William's feudal policy.[47] As soon as the feudal system prevailed throughout the West, Maine [48] long ago noted, it became evident that primogeniture had some great advantage over all other modes of succession. "It spread over Europe with remarkable rapidity," he [49] writes, "the principal instrument of diffusion being Family Settlements, the Pactes de Famille of France and Haus-Gesetze of Germany, which universally stipulated that lands held by knightly service should descend to the eldest son." In 1099 we find the rule in an Assize of Jerusalem, in 1158 in a rule of Frederick Barbarossa promulgated with respect to succession for Duchies, Courtships and Marquisates, and 1185 in Brittany.[50] But as Maine was quick to see, accounting for the diffusion of primogeniture by associating it with feudal policies was only half the problem. "For its origin," he [51] wrote in a famous passage, "the reason given does not account at all. Nothing in law springs entirely from the sense of convenience. There are always certain ideas existing antecedently on which the sense of convenience works, and of which it can do no more than form some new combination; and to find these ideas in the present case is exactly the problem." But we have learned from modern ethnology that these ideas, assuming their existence, are lost apparently beyond all hope of recovery. There is no evidence yet discovered which warrants us in going beyond the mere fact of diffusion. If we pass that point our conjecture at the most can amount to no more than a brilliant guess.

SOCIAL HEREDITY

By the term "social heredity" is meant the habits, knowledge, expedients, institutions, in brief, the culture, which is

[47] *Op. cit. supra* note 46, at 30.

[48] Maine, *op. cit. supra* note 5, at 192.

[49] *Ibid.*

[50] Kenney, *History of the Law of Primogeniture in England* (1878) 10 *et seq.*

[51] Maine, *op. cit. supra* note 5, at 193.

handed down from one generation to another by the processes
of teaching, learning or unconscious conditioning. Of the three
elements—invention, communication, social heredity—which
operate in the formation of culture, the latter is by far the
most important. All those mental characters which are specifically human, as Briffault has shown, are the products of social heredity. "Every step," he writes, "in human thought and
feeling is strictly determined by what went before. The bold-
est speculation of the thinker is bound within narrow limits
by the thought of his predecessors, and is the direct outcome
of an evolution which goes back in unbroken continuity to the
first flickerings of the human mind. Here, as elsewhere, evolution is gradual modification, not creation. No human sentiment, no idea, no institution has ever been created and made
its appearance suddenly and 'de novo.' " [52] All the social techniques and arts, all the folkways and institutions, which are
manifested in society are also a part of the social heritage. "If
the earth were struck by one of Mr. Wells's comets," Graham
Wallas [53] has written, "and if, in consequence, every human
being now alive were to lose all the knowledge and habits
which he had acquired from preceding generations (though
retaining unchanged all his own powers of invention, and
memory, and habituation) nine-tenths of the inhabitants of
London or New York would be dead in a month, and 99 per
cent of the remaining tenth would be dead in six months.
They would have no language to express their thoughts, and
no thoughts but vague reverie. They could not read notices,
or drive motors or horses. They would wander about, led by
the inarticulate cries of a few naturally dominant individuals,
drowning themselves, as thirst came on, in hundreds at the
riverside landing places, looting those shops where the smell
of decaying food attracted them, and perhaps at the end
stumbling on the expedient of cannibalism."

It is sometimes thought that the process of social heredity

[52] 1 Briffault, *The Mothers* (1927) 80.
[53] *Our Social Heritage* (1921) 16.

operates among certain sub-human species, but the evidence is inconclusive; furthermore, it violates the principle that, in attempting to explain animal behavior we should always do so on the lowest possible level, and refrain, unless under strictest compulsion, from imputing to them capacities of a high degree of complexity.[54] Thus in 1895, during a cold spring, a few sea-gulls discovered that by going up the Thames into the smoky atmosphere of London they could easily obtain food. Since then, large numbers of the gulls come to London every winter, in mild weather as well as cold. In view of the gradualness with which evolution operates in its biological aspects it is certain that the gulls have evolved no new biologically inherited instinct; but it does not follow that they have therefore acquired a new socially inherited habit. We may legitimately adopt a much simpler view, in which heredity is ruled out altogether. It is reasonable to suppose that some of the gulls which originally were in London in 1895 returned in the following year accompanied by other gulls for reasons of gregariousness or imitation and that this process has continued from year to year. Perhaps the only test which would establish conclusively that social heredity operated in the present example would be to show that none of the gulls appearing in any year had ever before been in London.

It is important also to recognize that the process of social heredity differs from that of biological inheritance not only in degree but in kind. From time to time it has been suggested that culture, or certain culture traits, are transmitted in the germ plasm. This is a view which has been put forward in recent years by Bateson, Gates and Conklin among others,[55] but the evidence to support it is completely lacking. All the evidence we possess points in fact towards the conclusion that

[54] *The Animal Mind* (1930) 36.

[55] Bateson, *Methods and Scope of Genetics* (1908) 34; Gates, *Heredity and Eugenics* (1920) 12 Eugenics Review 4; Conklin, *Heredity and Environment in the Development of Man* (1915) 306.

what is termed social heredity is transmitted essentially by the processes of teaching, learning and unconscious conditioning. The evidence for this view is overwhelming and has been collected with great industry by Briffault.[56] A simple imaginary example of McDougall [57] will illustrate the point. He suggests that if by a magical operation all the babies born to English parents were at once exchanged for infants born to French parents, so that the latter country had been secretly peopled by pure Englishmen, and England by Frenchmen, the exchange would produce practically no effect. "Faith comes by hearing." A man, as Briffault concludes, will be a Buddhist in China and a Quaker in Pennsylvania, by virtue of traditional, and not of racial, heredity. He will, on principle, be a polygamist in Persia, a monogamist in modern Europe. In the Congo he will "think cannibal thoughts." It is more accurate, in fact, to borrow an expression of Wallas, to say that we have become biologically parasitic upon our social heritage. We have become biologically more fitted to live with the aid of our social heritage, and biologically less fitted to live without it. A large part of the human race would, for example, quickly perish if, confined to its present geographical areas, it were deprived of clothing.

Law is both a part and a product of social heredity. It is a part of the culture into which every individual is born and as such exercises a modifying influence on human behavior and human thought. It is also a product of the process of traditional inheritance. Through the mechanics of teaching and learning, the law of one generation is transmitted to the succeeding generation. Maitland has referred to the toughness of a taught tradition. Strictly, all traditions are taught, but law, at all events in advanced societies, in common with at least one other form of social control, religion, possesses the marked characteristic of a professional body of thinkers, who preserve

[56] *The Mothers*, ch. II *passim*.
[57] *An Introduction to Social Psychology* (1923) 337.

and pass on the ideas associated with it. This is a condition
which obviously makes for "toughness." Wigmore [58] is in-
clined even to make it a necessary condition of the survival of
legal systems, perhaps limiting the term "legal system" to the
complex forms found in the more developed cultures. "The
principal feature that controls the creation or the survival of a
legal system," he writes, "is the rise and persistence of a body
of technical legal ideas; and this body of legal ideas is itself
the result of the existence of a professional class of legal
thinkers or practitioners, who created and preserved the body
of ideas independently of the identity of the political system
and independently of the purity of the race-stock. In short,
the rise and perpetuation of a legal system is dependent on
the development and survival of a highly trained professional
class." The existence of experts, as we can observe, is certainly not a necessary condition for the existence of the rudimentary systems of law found in primitive communities; it
would appear, for reasons which will readily occur, that the
perpetuation of any complex and detailed system, whether it
be law, mathematics or architecture, is dependent upon the
existence of experts with a knowledge of the system. Even
relatively simple arts, such as canoe building, the manufac-
ture of pottery and bows and arrows, disappear completely,
notwithstanding a vital need for their continuance, when the
skilled craftsmen who have carried on the industry die out.[59]

Two characteristics are noticeable in the operation of the
process of social inheritance. The first is the tendency for it to
accumulate and the second is a tendency towards modification. At any given time in a society the processes of invention
and diffusion are at work, if only feebly, as in the case of the
so-called "stationary peoples," and thus by a general method
of accretion the content of culture is constantly increased. At
present in the United States, the body of law, both statutory

[58] *Panorama of the World's Legal Systems* (1936) 1129.
[59] Rivers, *The Disappearance of Useful Arts* (1912) in Festskrift Til-
lägnad Edvard Westermarck.

and judicial, is increasing at a rate perhaps never before equaled in any other society in history. In the absence of some sweeping reform, revolutionary or otherwise, the vast bulk of law invented by the present generation, together with the greater bulk it has received from past generations, will be passed on to generations yet unborn. But it is certain that those generations will not be content to accept it without modification, just as the present generation has adapted the law transmitted to it. It is perhaps the most familiar characteristic of the legal process. Originally it made no difference, for example, with respect to the validity of a will that the testator after its execution had married and had issue. Later, however, the courts viewed these facts as having a significance on the question of implied revocation of a will of personalty. Soon a rule was laid down that they created a presumption of revocation. For a short while a distinction was made as to wills of land, but it later was held that the presumption applied with equal force to wills of land and personalty. Still later, the presumption became a rule of law, so that if there were a marriage and subsequent birth of issue these facts of themselves were held to have the legal effect of revocation. Finally, at least one jurisdiction has now held that a will made subsequent to a marriage but prior to birth of issue is revoked by the birth of issue.[60]

To summarize, culture and all the elements comprising culture, including law, are the product of invention, borrowing or social heredity. These three factors may function singly or in combination, but the culture of any society of which we have knowledge is the product of all three. It has been shown also that culture traits previously unknown are the product solely of invention. That is to say, when a culture trait is pursued to its point of origin it will be found that it originated in man's ingenuity. This ingenuity may be of an elementary

[60] Karr v. Robinson 167 Md. 375, 173 Atl. 584 (1934); Dickinson, *Administrative Justice* (1927) 204.

kind, as in an unconsciously perceived method of invention and trial; or it may be more advanced, as in purposeful reflective thought; but in any case the ultimate root of any single culture trait is invention.

4.

THE PRINCIPLE OF DISORDER

THE CONCEPTION THAT CULTURE is ultimately a product of the process of invention cannot be too strongly emphasized. It is one of the ideas which frees the social sciences from the dominance of the mechanistic theories of the Seventeenth and Eighteenth Centuries. The mechanistic conception of the world put forward in the century of Newton corrupted at its base our whole theory of social science. It almost stifled progress in this field by setting it in a direction which led to a blind end.

To the ancient question "What is the world made of?" the Seventeenth Century answered, "The world is a succession of instantaneous configurations of matter,—or of material, if you wish to include stuff more subtle than ordinary matter, the ether for example." [1] Although every configuration of matter was regarded as distinct from every other, they were nevertheless held to be causally related to one another. Newton and his disciples, in other words, regarded the world as subject to the reign of law; there was a definite order in nature. The idea of the order of nature is, as Whitehead has shown, a local belief; it possesses a history which can be discovered. He has traced the idea to the medieval insistence on a rational, personal, energetic god. Let us assume that such a being is

[1] Whitehead, *Science and the Modern World* (1925) 71.

responsible for the universe, then it is a reasonable inference, or so it appeared to the medieval mind, that the universe is constructed on a rational plan and will exhibit elements of order and congruity. The Newtonian discoveries came as a great confirmation of this theological belief.

"All are but parts of one stupendous whole,
Whose body Nature is, and God the soul."

The order of nature is one of our own most fundamental assumptions, yet it does not seem part of the mental equipment of the people of Asia, perhaps because they possessed no god similar to the god of Medieval Europe. But, to Western thought in the Seventeenth and succeeding centuries, nature appeared as essentially orderly and rational. This idea appealed to the imagination of the educated classes and spread with amazing swiftness. More important, the Seventeenth Century world scheme became the most perfect instrument of research yet devised by man. The mechanical explanation of the processes of Nature became, by virtue of its unparalleled triumphs, a dogma of science. Today, in philosophy and science, its limitations are recognized. Clerk Maxwell was perhaps the last scientist of the first rank to devote painstaking efforts to a reconciliation of mechanical theory with modern developments of physics.

The almost miraculous achievements of mechanism in science led to the immediate adoption of the theory in social thought and jurisprudence. Hobbes, Leibnitz, Pufendorf and Grotius [2] among others attempted to base their systems of law directly upon it. In jurisprudence, it came to the foreground again in the first half of the Nineteenth Century with the general revival of the mathematico-physical point of view.[3]

[2] *Cf.* the writer's book, *Law and the Social Sciences* (1935) 129 for a further analysis of the mechanistic movement in Seventeenth Century jurisprudence.

[3] Pound, *Jurisprudence* in *History and Prospects of the Social Sciences* (1925) 458; Korkunov, *General Theory of Law* (1922) 259.

In the social sciences generally, particularly economics and sociology, it even now occupies a dominant position. Although, in most cases, simple mechanical explanations have been abandoned, the related notions of order and stability still prevail. Only rarely are they explicitly recognized, but implicit in most economic and sociological thought is the belief that there is an ultimate economic or social order, analogous to or a part of the order of nature, which it is the business of the economist or sociologist to discover. At the basis of social thought today is the Holbachian view that man is the work of nature; he exists in nature; he is submitted to her laws; he cannot deliver himself from them.

Three centuries of failure should teach us to look in new directions. In physical science the concept of nature is undergoing profound transformations, although the idea still prevails, and perhaps rightly, that physical laws are evidence of a certain general characteristic of orderliness in the phenomena of nature. It is advisable also for social thought to reëxamine its own basic concepts, particularly those which it has taken over from mechanism. A general atmosphere of patience and expectancy marks current social thought. In modern times it secured its first real impetus by the process of borrowing apparently suitable concepts from mechanism during the period of the rise of that movement. Physical science again appears to be entering upon a period of wider triumphs and a deeper revelation of the secrets of the external world. Each step in the apparent progress of physical science is anxiously studied by the social theorist in the hope that by clinging to the coattails of the new physical ideas social thought itself will be carried to new and more advanced levels. There is no evidence, however, that ideas which illuminate the nature of matter or of physical relations will throw any light on social life or social relations. The available evidence points in fact to the conclusion that social thought must take its origin in concepts which are, at any rate today, the antithesis of the basic ideas of physical science.

Starting from a mechanistic base, social thinkers have developed the notion that social life is essentially orderly and congruous. Perhaps even in the absence of the theories of mechanism, the idea would have occurred to social philosophers. All societies upon inspection appear to exhibit elements of orderliness and congruity. There is, however, an essential difference between the so-called order of nature and the order which we observe in society. The former is given; the latter must be attained; that is to say, the physical scientist may assume the order of nature as part of the data of experience. The laws which he develops explain, in a more or less intelligible manner, the order which is assumed as part of the data. In social theory, however, no such assumption is warranted. The products of social life, which may be conveniently summed up in the label "culture," are inventions. Social life and social relations are, in other words, basically incongruous and disorderly. The order which we observe in society is an invention of man; it is not something in its myriad forms which automatically surrounds him, but it must be achieved. Whatever may be the case in nature, order in social life is wrought from disorder.[4]

Human energy manifests itself in a complex variety of forms which almost defy analysis. The springs of that energy are even more varied than the forms which result. No systematic classification of them would dare omit as beyond the limits of possibility any part of the world which has revealed itself to man. This is an ancient view, one common to the philosophies of all ages, and needs no elaboration. The oneness of the universe is something that has always been imagined, even if its demonstration still remains to be accomplished. The human world is thus one of infinite complexity. It includes not only the physical universe but the even more diverse world of the human mind and of human relations.

[4] This approach was first developed by L. K. Frank, *The Principle of Disorder and Incongruity in Economic Affairs*, Political Science Quarterly, December, 1932.

Upon every human being there impinges, in addition to material factors, a vast complex of social systems and institutions, wishes, desires, impulses, attitudes, interests, thoughts, traditions, appetites and passions, and all the multitudinous combinations of these forces.

Whether or not these factors, if left unchecked, would produce any of the types of orderly societies of which we have knowledge is a question we cannot answer and need not put forward. Such a question belongs in the same class with the problem of the ape, endowed with perpetual life and seated before a typewriter, who will, so the mathematics of probability assure us, reproduce eventually the complete works of Shakespeare. Another factor enters which obviates all necessity for the question. The forces which operate in the human world are not, in fact, left unchecked. They are impeded in their free operations by the modifying or canceling effects of one another and, more importantly, by intentional controls invented by man. A particular type of order may be discovered accidentally by the method of invention and trial, or it may be achieved intentionally by the method of deliberate control; it may even be reached, in a rough and imperfect form, as was shown in an earlier chapter, as an inevitable feature of group life. But, in any event, the order which exists in human society at any given time is predominantly an achieved order, an invention at the center of which is man; it is not the order of the physical universe, which in physical theory is the product of the blind operation of nature and has always obtained or was established in the form apparent to us countless ages ago.

In social theory, therefore, order cannot, as in physical theory, be assumed as part of the data. A large part of the social theorist's task is the explanation of the achievement of order in society. He cannot take for granted, as the physical theorist may in his analogous sphere, an ultimate social order which it is his task to discover. He must assume an ultimate disorder, which through the agency of man's inventiveness and other factors has been changed into order.

It is well to set forth here precisely as may be what is meant by disorder. Order is defined above as a relationship among elements of the kind that when we know the characteristics of certain of the elements, the characteristics of the remaining elements are indicated. Numerous systems of order exist in the societies, all operating to ensure certain kinds of behavior on the part of the individuals of which they are composed. Disorder means merely the failure of human beings to conform to such systems of order. Bergson [5] has taken the position that disorder as an absolute is an impossibility, that whenever we are confronted with what apparently is disorder, we are in reality faced with a different kind of order. We are interested, for example, upon entering a room in an order that is "willed"; we find, however, that the furniture in the room is disarranged, is disordered. Nevertheless the objects in the room exhibit an "automatic" order, although, inasmuch as we are not looking for it, we may not be aware of it. The position of each object in the room may be explained by the automatic movements of the person who has slept in the room, or by the other efficient factors, whatever they may be, that have caused each article of furniture to be where it is; the order, in the second sense of the word, is perfect. From this point of view, disorder, in the sense of there being no order at all, is not to be found in any imaginable society. But one of the main characteristics of social science, and particularly law, is its exclusive teleological character. Law is primarily a system of order, a system of purposefully controlled human conduct. In the absence of all purposeful social controls, "automatic" order in the Bergsonian sense would still exist in society; but it would not exist from the teleological standpoint of social science. Order in social thought must always be approached from the point of view of desires and

[5] *Creative Evolution* (1913) 232.

interests of the individuals and groups comprising the society. When human behavior does not conform to the established systems of control, there is disorder in the society.

The ideal of science is the systematic interrelation of facts. Its progress is in the direction of generality and certainty. In the legal field, there is ample room for many types of investigations. In general, the types of investigation which have principally occupied jurists have been concerned with the analysis of the nature of the legal system. The importance of such investigations cannot be overemphasized. If we are engaged in discussing something, we cannot know too well what it is we are discussing. Contemporary juristic thought, convinced that it knows well the nature of what it is discussing, now emphasizes reform. This too, as a type of investigation, is important, although there is room for skepticism of such a program when the anticipated results of any serious reform rest not upon knowledge but upon sheer conjecture. It is here that the principle of disorder becomes a vital factor in legal thought. It provides a point of departure for a systematic interconnection of legal facts. It relates those facts to social facts generally, and it connects jurisprudence with the other social sciences devoted to the study of human behavior. Above all, it directs attention to the central fact of social life, namely, that it is essentially incongruous and disorderly. In the elimination of that incongruity and disorder, no factor plays a more important part than law. But the principle of disorder tells us that the existence of order in society is the product of purposeful control and, as such, is capable of change and manipulation in accordance with the capacities and imagination of man.

5.

THE INVENTIVE PROCESS

DISORDER DIRECTS ATTENTION TO the fact that the harmonious character of social life is an achievement of man and is not given. This concept liberates us from the shallow mechanism which seeks to explain the motion of human affairs by parallels drawn from physics. It does not, however, eliminate the possibility that human conduct is not solely the result of the free rationality of man but is the product in some degree of factors external to man. Superficial analogies based upon mechanistic concepts, such as the so-called "law of social gravitation," will not aid us in the search for these external contributing factors. Social thought, while utilizing the essentials of scientific method and having as its goal the general ideal of the exact sciences, must devise its own concepts. A department of knowledge dependent for its general ideas upon workers in other fields is barren at its core.

Law at its ultimate source, as we have seen, is an invention, which we have defined as the creation by man of new forms or processes. Despite the care with which the subject has been studied, the inventive process still remains obscure. It is no solution of the problem to assert, as Montmasson [1]

[1] *Invention and the Unconscious* (1932) *passim.*

does, that all invention is the product of the unconscious. An unconscious thinker demands just as much explanation as a conscious thinker; it is no step towards clarification to posit such hypothetical entities. The general pattern of the inventive process as it has been developed by psychological experiment and analysis is, first, awareness of a need, second, reflection upon the need, third, a sudden illumination, and, finally, painstaking efforts to perfect the insight.[2] All the steps appear essential but none more so than the demand for previous acquaintance with the subject matter. Hamilton's discovery of quaternions came to him "like a flash" while on a walk with his wife; but for the past fifteen years much of his energy had been devoted to a solution of this problem. In a recent illuminating study of the psychology of the inventor not a case is found in which the person who produced a valuable invention was unacquainted with the field of his contribution.[3]

Different psychological investigators tend to emphasize different steps in the act of discovery. Graham Wallas,[4] utilizing the earlier researches of Helmholtz, divides the process into four stages: Preparation, the stage during which the problem was investigated in all directions; Incubation, the stage during which the investigator was not consciously thinking about the problem; Illumination, the stage which consists of the appearance of the "happy idea" together with the psychological events which immediately preceded and accompanied that appearance. Of his own case Helmholtz remarked that "they came particularly readily during the slow ascent of wooded hills on a sunny day," and Rémy de Gourmont observed, "My conceptions rise into the field of consciousness like a flash of lightning or the flight of a bird." Long be-

[2] Murphy, *General Psychology* (1933) 422 *et seq.*; Spearman, *Creative Mind* (1931) 105 *et seq.*; Rignano, *Psychology of Reasoning* (1923) c. vi; Woodworth, *Dynamic Psychology* (1918) c. vi.

[3] Rossman, *The Psychology of the Inventor* (1931).

[4] *The Art of Thought* (1926) 80 *et seq.*

fore, Plato had pointed out in the *Symposium* that "He who has been instructed thus far in the things of love, and has learned to see beautiful things in due order and succession, when he comes to the end, will suddenly perceive a beauty wonderful in its nature." Wallas added a fourth stage, Verification, which Helmholtz did not mention. By this he means the period in which both the validity of the idea was tested, and the idea itself was reduced to exact form. All that we can hope from inspirations, Poincaré[5] concluded, is to obtain points of departure for lengthy calculations, involving discipline, attention, will, and, consequently, consciousness.

Benjamin[6] makes the important point that the *discovery* which is usually referred to is of *hypotheses* rather than *data*. He is careful to point out that this is not to say that the scientist does not discover facts. He remarks:

> The discovery of facts occurs in science in two important ways—prior to the formulation of hypotheses, and after such formulation. In the former type, the discovery is primarily due to the data rather than to the scientist; the data impress themselves upon his attention because of their obviousness, or because of their intensity, or because of their unusual character, or because of some other more or less accidental factor. But in the latter type, the data are discovered through the instrumentality of the theory; because the scientist has, through freely creative activities of the imagination, devised a theory having certain definitely predictable consequences, he is able to anticipate what nature will reveal in certain definitely specified localities. He then turns his observation to these areas and discovers what occurs. But the data thus discovered might have remained unknown had it not been for the directed attention; hence their discovery is a result of the theoretical activity of the scientist. For this

[5] *Science and Method* (1914) 75.

[6] *Philosophy of Science* (1937) 173. By permission of The Macmillan Company, publishers. *Logical Structure of Science* (1936) 303 *et seq.*

reason the real problem in this connection centers about the discovery of the hypothetical and theoretical notions which are to serve as the guiding factors in observation. The mystery in science is not how one discovers facts which are obvious, but how one discovers theories which in turn enable him to discover facts which are not obvious.

Although psychological investigation has been directed in the main to the study of creative imagination as it has displayed itself in men of genius, there is no reason to suppose that the inventive process is essentially different when manifested on lower levels or by men of lesser capacity. In the ordering of human relations, as in other spheres, creative imagination is a necessary factor. Sometimes in the social world, its products—such as the invention of the concept of intangible property—are on a level with its highest accomplishments of mechanical, literary or artistic creation. But in all cases it seems to follow the general pattern of recognition of a need, reflection, illumination, and patient development.

In the creation of a legal system, however, the steps just outlined represent only the general case and are subject to many exceptions in detail. It does not cover, for example, the arbitrary decrees of an insane despot, such as those of the Fourteenth Century Milanese ruler, Giovanni Maria Visconti. Aristotle's contention that such decrees represent a temporary suspension of legal rule is merely a device of democratic propaganda; since the decrees are operative in practice, and frequently for long periods of time, it would be absurd, sociologically, to deny them the status of legality. Nevertheless, in spite of such exceptions the general pattern is plain enough and, for most cases, appears accurately to describe the facts. Its weakness, however, is that it is merely a description of a process and not an explanation. We are compelled to look elsewhere for the explanation, although always keeping before us the main outlines of the process itself.

THE THEORY OF FORCES

A possible explanation appears to lie in the concept of "force." In other words, "forces" operating in society may create circumstances which permit the inventive process to function in the development of a legal system. Possible sources of such "forces" are inanimate nature, organisms other than man, and man himself.

The concept of force, in its explicit employment, was borrowed by social thinkers from physics. Traces of the idea may perhaps be found in Plato and Aristotle, and in Aquinas. In Herbert Spencer the notion almost became explicit, and in Lester Ward it at last crystallized. Since the appearance of Ward's writings the concept has been one of the mainstays of American sociological thought. It cannot be said that social thinkers have been any happier than the physicists in their handling of the notion. It is sometimes asserted that the idea arose from the effort of pushing, throwing or pulling; from the muscular sensation accompanying each of these acts. Such an assertion cannot, of course, be verified and is therefore only a conjecture. Nevertheless, an indication of the sensational basis of the scientific concept of force is a useful device to convey its meaning to the uninitiated. We should be careful, however, in employing the idea to purify it of all elements of anthropomorphism; otherwise we may be misled into serious errors. Classical philosophy wasted much effort in an attempt to determine whether force was a *vis a tergo* or a *vis a fronte* (a push or a pull). We certainly feel a strain when we lift a chair from the floor; but we cannot mean that the moon feels such a strain in its raising of the tides on the earth. The concept of force when unpurified of anthropomorphism is, as Tyler remarked, "the last remnant of fetichism in modern physics."

Force is defined in physics as equal to mass times acceleration $(f=m\ a)$. This equation, which was given by Newton, is the basic equation of mechanics. Whether or not force in this sense has any real existence is still disputed. Descartes touched upon the vitally important idea that weight, velocity and "an infinite number of similar instances" [7] were mathematical dimensions of motion, just as length, depth and breadth are dimensions of extension. If he had developed the idea our whole thinking in physics might have been different. Russell asserts that "force is a mathematical fiction, not a physical entity";[8] but our lingering traces of anthropomorphism incline us to be skeptical. The essential thing, however, is that force is measurable in terms of mass, although this latter concept is itself extremely obscure.

In social theory, forces are generally thought of as the psychic incentives to behavior, the urges which impel individuals to act. Many such impulses have been suggested—desires, instincts, wishes, wants and satisfactions, values, predispositions, interests, attitudes and tendencies, and numerous others. Whether or not the notion sociologists have of these incentives differs vitally from the comparable physical notion is not clear. It has been suggested that the application of physical force must result in the occurrence of some kind of change; and that psychic force is stimulative but is not necessarily followed by change. Assuming that such an idea of physical force is a part of physical theory, it does not follow that the suggested distinction is sound. Psychic force may not, and in most instances does not, result in change occurring in the world. By the admission, however, of those who suggest the distinction, change in the human organism is always the outcome of psychic force. It is "stimulating" to the organism. That is indubitably a "change." Whether the impulses of the psychic forces have further limits is another question. There are limits to the observable effects of forces operating in the physical world, and there are corresponding limits in the realm of the psychic forces.

It is apparent that when the sociologist speaks of "social

[7] 1 *Philosophical Works of Descartes* (1911) 61.
[8] *Principles of Mathematics* (2nd ed. 1938) 482.

forces" and the psychologist of "drives" or "motives" they are talking of the same thing. The problem of human motivation has been the source of one of the major controversies of modern psychology. From time to time attempts have been made to settle the question on a monistic basis. McDougall explained all motivation in terms of instincts and emotions; Pareto isolated the "residue" as the prime mover and developed an elaborate classification of the various kinds. Freud was one of the first to reveal the complexity of the problem and the likelihood that no easy answer could be expected. The speculative flights which psychology has permitted itself have no doubt had their uses; but its present-day emphasis on the experimental method is a desirable corrective. "Scientific psychology is a part of physics, or the study of nature; it is the record of how animals act," Santayana has written. "Literary psychology is the art of imagining how they feel and think." Both methods have their places but the first seems to provide us greater certainty and more possibility of usefulness, so far at any rate as the present problem is concerned. Observation and laboratory experiments are centered now on the types of human behavior which appear to be capable of measurement —hunger, thirst, fear, memory, etc. Much is now known of these phenomena; but we still lack sufficient knowledge of them to be employed as the basis of a general theory of human behavior or a general theory of society.

At bottom the theory of social forces represents an effort to account for social phenomena upon the basis of psychic experiences. Our knowledge, however, of such experiences is too scanty to permit us to expect any real illumination from the theory. We have no precise understanding of the nature of a wish, a desire, an interest or any of the numerous psychic urges which have been classified as social forces. Ward's statement that "all beings which can be said to perform actions do so in obedience to those mental states which are denominated desires" [9] would seem to rule out all other psychic

[9] 1 *Dynamic Sociology* (2nd ed. 1923) 468.

urges and to constitute desires as the sole causative agent. Assuming that we had a clear conception of the nature of desire, we still fall short of a satisfactory explanation of human behavior; we are not told what prompts the desire. To assert that human beings have children because of a philoprogenitive desire tells us nothing, any more than the "dormative principle" of opium in Molière's travesty of scholasticism conveys any explanation. It is exceedingly unlikely that any general principles can be deduced from the theory as it now stands and the analytical difficulties it creates are almost insuperable. Moreover, it scarcely seems from the standpoint of the possibility of productive results that the theory possesses sufficient intrinsic merit to warrant the undertaking of the necessarily arduous and extensive analysis required. It is plain that the psychic urges which have been posited were in large part, if not entirely, invented to explain human action; and it is even plainer that when we pass beyond mere redundancy we have no explanation at all. We have admittedly, in other words, except for a self-serving assertion, failed to isolate the determining factor.

CAUSATION

Nor are we further advanced if we turn directly to the doctrine of causation. The theory of social forces is part of the wider principle of causation, and many of the problems of the former must wait for their solution upon the final disposition of those of the latter. Unfortunately the day that will witness this event seems far distant. Although, as Cohen has pointed out, the idea of cause took its origin in the field of legal procedure—a cause (αἰτία) being the ground for an action—it is the philosophers and not the lawyers who have brought the notion to its present unhappy state.

Hume's argument that to exist is to be experienced, and that as no causal relationship is ever experienced there is none, has left philosophers hopelessly at odds. Russell today takes very much the same position that Hume took and is attacked quite as vigorously as Hume was. The present dispute oscillates around his assertion that causal laws express nothing but regularities of sequence. He argues that the word "cause" is so inextricably bound up with misleading associations as to make its complete extrusion from the philosophical vocabulary desirable; that, in fact, laws of probable sequence of the type contemplated by Mill, though useful in the infancy of science, are displaced later by laws, the constancy of which consists in a "sameness of relations" or a "sameness of differential equations." The difficulty with Russell's view that causal laws express nothing but regularities of sequence is that it appears to lead to paradoxical conclusions. Thus night will be the cause of day and day the cause of night. Similarly, the blowing of the factory whistle is the cause of the position of the hands of the clock when the men begin to leave the factory for dinner, and the blowing of the whistle in a New York factory causes both the departure of the men from that factory and also the departure of the men from factories in Philadelphia and in Baltimore, and conversely. There are other objections to Russell's theory. If B always follows A, there are three possible interpretations: (i) A is the cause of B; (ii) some other thing, X, is the cause of B; (iii) it is the result of coincidence. Our ignorance of the ultimate nature of this process is complete.

It is evident that we shall have to wait long for positive assistance from philosophy. Other methods of handling the problem of causation have been developed which may bear fruit for the legal theorist and sociologist; but we are at too early a stage in their development to possess any certain convictions. We can think of a cause, perhaps, as the single element which is present in the case in which the result occurs and which is not present in the case in which it does not occur.[10] Seeds from the same plant, for example, are sown in

[10] For an analysis of this view of causation see Jennings, *Causes and Determiners in Radically Experimental Analysis* (1913) 47 The American Naturalist 349. For a comprehensive account of the doctrine of causality in modern physics, see Lindsay and Morgenau, *Foundations of Physics* (1936) c. x. For its position in philosophy see Ducasse, *Causation and the Types of Necessity* (1924).

two adjacent fields, the soils of which are identical except that one is alkaline and the other acid. Plants grow from the seeds in the alkaline field but not in the acid field. The alkalinity of the soil is thus the "cause" of the appearance of the plant. Assuming the validity of such a view it seems unlikely that its successful adoption in the realm of social phenomena is possible. Too many elements are present in every social event for us to be certain that we have selected the true determiner. The most successful application of this method is to be found unquestionably in Toynbee's monumental work, *A Study of History*. From his vast historical knowledge he appears to be able to select cases in which only the crucial factors vary. A fair sample is his comparison of Attica and Boeotia. We are all familiar with the contrast between the cultivated Athenian and the rustic Boeotian lout. Toynbee accounts for these different products of neighboring countries by the difference between their soils. That of Boeotia is deep and easy of cultivation, it leads to a life of ease; that of Attica is abnormally light and stony, it calls for strenuous efforts on the part of its inhabitants. The Boeotian existed almost without effort, and art and philosophy and science hardly touched him. The Athenian wrestled with his soil and produced olive oil which he was forced to dispose of in the markets of the world. Thus a chain was created—exports, industries, merchant ships, money, a navy, command of the sea—the links of which lead to the political, artistic and intellectual culture which made Athens "the education of Hellas." It is a theory of great plausibility but among the large number of possible factors we have no guaranty that the determining factor has been chosen. The slightly superior geographical position of Attica may be the true determiner. It is significant that Corinth, which also achieved a high civilization, enjoyed geographical advantages similar to Attica. How a slight geographic advantage may be turned to great account we witness in England in the era of the Stuarts when her inhabitants made her the center of the new transoceanic commerce and of the economic system that

sustained it. Either account of the supremacy of Attica over Boeotia may be correct or both may be wrong. Our difficulty in the present state of our knowledge is that we have not yet devised a method which will permit us to bring any view to a conclusive test.

Moreover, we tend now to recognize, although again following the lead of physical theory, the enormous complexity of the phenomena which we are attempting to analyze. Because of its inadequateness, physics has slowly abandoned the Newtonian concept of matter, which held that each bit of matter was fully describable without reference to any other portion of matter. "Modern physics," Whitehead [11] has written, "has abandoned the doctrine of Simple Location. The physical things which we term stars, planets, lumps of matter, molecules, electrons, protons, quanta of energy, are each to be conceived as modifications of conditions within space time, extending throughout its whole range. There is a focal region, which in common speech is where the thing is. But its influence streams away from it with finite velocity throughout the utmost recesses of space and time." Perhaps modern social theory should also abandon all efforts to work out a tenable hypothesis of social causation. Such a position has been strongly and convincingly urged by Pareto and others. Society appears to be the product of an enormous number of factors which can perhaps be grouped under the general categories: environmental, biological, psychological and cultural. Changes in and interaction of the elements of these factors seem to produce noticeable social changes and no factor appears determinative of social change as a whole; that is to say, social change, we may be reasonably confident, is not the sole product of economic alterations, as Marx [12] thought it was, nor is it the result solely of technological adaptation, as Veblen [13] insisted. When we attempt to interpret a change even in one element of society,

[11] *Adventures of Ideas* (1933) 220 *et seq.*
[12] *Critique of Political Economy* (1859) Introduction.
[13] *The Theory of the Leisure Class* (1912) c. 8.

we find, if we look attentively, that many factors possibly are involved. Society appears too complex for us in most cases to explain a social trait as the "effect" of a single "cause," even assuming that the phrase "cause and effect" can be given an operative meaning.

OTHER THEORIES

We need not linger long over other traditional methods which might be adapted to throw light on the inventive process. Social evolution, the comparative method as employed by the classical anthropologists and as extended by statistical correlation, the method of rigorous ethnology, these and many others have been utilized in investigations of unquestionable value and no doubt contain elements of truth. Their present weaknesses, however, are readily apparent and generally recognized and it is unlikely that the adoption of any of them, whether singly or in combination, could lead to new general knowledge. The intensive study and application which social thinkers of immense capacity have devoted to them makes it appear that their utilization at this late date could put us in possession only of results which are already known. Similarly, results of great value may some day be expected from the further development of the logic of discovery which is concerned with the operations of classifying, ordering and correlating events, and the technique of hypothesis formation.[14] In its present stage, however, it is only of elementary assistance.

We must rest content, at this point of the development of our inquiry, with the knowledge that law and culture are inventions. We possess a knowledge of the general pattern of the inventive process but our knowledge of the circumstances

[14] Benjamin, *Philosophy of Science*, 181 *et. seq.*; Carmichael, *The Logic of Discovery* (1930); Gore, *Scientific Discovery* (1871) 355 *et seq.*; Tyndall, *Scientific Use of the Imagination* in *Fragments of Science* (2nd ed. 1871) 125.

which call it into being is hypothetical, scanty and unreliable. No way seems immediately open to us to attack the problem directly. We must hope for success through an indirect solution. We must study what has been invented in the hope that thereby we shall discover why it was invented.

6.

THE METHOD OF LEGAL SCIENCE

In order to study what has been invented it is necessary to determine first what methods we shall employ. The task of jurisprudence consists of the examination of the realm of law and the formulation of valid propositions. We must therefore adopt methods of research and procedure which seem likely to permit us to reach this desired end. We cannot tell in advance whether or not the methods we adopt will have this result; such devices as we employ will thus be merely methodological assumptions. There will be ample occasion to give them a critical foundation if they reveal any success.

HYPOTHESIS AND VERIFICATION

The general method which seems desirable is that of hypothesis and verification, with such assistance as the more individualized methods can render. Modern empiricism is opposed to this view and insists that we should begin with the facts. Two problems, however, immediately suggest themselves. What is meant by a fact? and, What facts are we to study? We may postpone consideration of the first question until later, as it is one which must be answered no matter what view of methodology we take, and which will be answered in accordance with the view which we take. What facts are we to study? Obviously we have neither the time nor the energy to study all the facts. A telephone book contains a great many facts, but it is not likely that it would lead to fruitful knowledge for jurisprudence to segregate them all. The number of facts in the external world is beyond human enumeration and the investigator must employ some method of segregation and indulge in some assumptions. As to the latter, at the very least he assumes that the external world exists and that the study of a portion of it will lead to knowledge. As to the former, any method of segregation must involve an hypothesis of what is relevant. Even the empiricist does not study all the facts; he studies only the facts which appear to have relevance or which seem to be crucial; but in approaching these latter facts he inescapably indulges in hypothetical thinking. "The most reckless and treacherous of all theorists," Marshall [1] pointedly observed, "is he who professes to let facts and figures speak for themselves." The unsatisfactory condition of the branch of astronomy devoted to the study of long-period variable stars is an illustration of the result of permitting facts to speak for themselves. In that field we have, perhaps as nearly as may be, the naked fact speaking for itself: namely, the length of a light cycle. But the naked fact, in this instance at any rate, remains obstinately mute. It reveals only what is already known, namely, that there is a great variation in brightness and that the cycle of light change is only roughly periodic. Progress in that field has taken place only when the facts have been approached from the point of view of a problem. The hypothesis, for example, that the variability of the long-period variable Omicron Ceti is due to internal oscillations was found to be supported by measurements of the changes in its radial velocity. The history of science bears ample witness to the truth that the development of knowledge is dependent upon the formation of fruitful hypotheses; and that scientific method itself is merely

[1] Pigou (ed.) *Memorials of Alfred Marshall* (1925) 108.

72   THE THEORY OF LEGAL SCIENCE

the means by which we endeavor to answer the questions
raised by hypotheses.

By the term hypothesis is meant a proposition which is asserted for the purposes of study without any suggestion as to
its truth or falsity. By definition a proposition is a sentence
which expresses that which is true or false, but in the case of
hypotheses we suspend judgment until such time as the study
has been completed. Cassirer [2] has insisted that two methods
are open to us in science. "We can, by a pure 'abstractive'
method," he writes, "separate from a group of given things or
phenomena that group of determinations which is common to
all members of the class, and which belongs to them directly
in their sensuous appearance; or we can go behind the phenomena to certain *hypotheses* for the explanation of the field
of physical facts in question. Only the first procedure strictly
corresponds to the demands of scientific and philosophic criticism. For only here are we sure that we do not falsify the observations of arbitrary interpretation; only here do we remain
purely in the field of the facts themselves, for while we divide
the facts into definite classes, we add no foreign feature to
them." Cassirer is merely drawing a distinction between descriptive and explanatory science. This difference is usually
expressed by stating that descriptive science answers the question "How?" and explanatory science the question "Why?"
The law of falling bodies tells us how they fall, not why. The
realm of descriptive science is the realm of the brute fact; we
know the subject matter exists, but we do not know why. We
need not stop to ask whether, on this basis, a descriptive
science is really a science, for as Benjamin has pointed out,
there are probably no such sciences in existence. Meteorology,
which probably most closely approaches the ideal of descriptive science, is in such an unsatisfactory state that it is incon-
ceivable it could inspire any spirit of emulation. The processes

[2] *Substance and Function and Einstein's Theory of Relativity* (1923)
193. To the same effect see also Bavink, *The Natural Sciences* (1932)
42; Dingle, *Science and Human Experience* (1931) 22.

of ordering, classifying and correlating are no doubt essential operations in scientific method, but to say that they are the end of science is to ignore most, if not all, the advances which the history of science reveals to us. That history discloses that a science "must contain hypotheses, theories and conjectures; it must make predictions; it must experiment; it must attempt to get behind or beneath phenomena to discover their deeper features and their essential connections." [3] Hypotheses bring to the scrutiny of brute facts the additional content which makes possible scientific development. "The growth of science," as Whitehead has observed, "is not primarily in bulk but in ideas." We must also recognize that the facts do not suggest the appropriate hypothesis. "The history of science," Cohen has sensitively remarked, "indicates rather that fruitful hypotheses have generally come to certain gifted minds as musical themes or great poetic expressions have come to others. You may call them the gift of the gods to their favorites." The hypothesis is "the leap into the unknown," the insight beyond appearance which takes us to reality.

Jurisprudence today stands in great need of more hypotheses. "We have too little theory in the law rather than too much," Holmes wrote a generation ago, and the condition which he was criticizing has not since improved. All the hypotheses which jurists have been able to invent have been found to be inconsistent with the facts. This has not injured the hypotheses, but has resulted in a denial of the facts or an assumption that they are unworthy of notice. The chief American expounder during the last generation of the command theory of law took great care to warn his readers that his hypothesis was "a purely juristic one," i.e., it was completely contrary to the facts. In scientific method hypothesis represents only one half of the scissors; verification is the indispensable remaining half.

The problem of verification presents innumerable difficul-

[3] Benjamin, *An Introduction to the Philosophy of Science* (1937) 145.

ties, both in the theory of knowledge and in scientific method. In legal science, as Yntema [4] observed some years ago, it is becoming crucial. Two processes appear, however, to be involved in making a verification: (1) the process of deduction and (2) the process of confirmation.

One of the formal conditions of an hypothesis is that it must be so framed that deductions capable of confirmation or disproof can be made from it; otherwise it is empirically meaningless. It should be observed, however, as Carnap [5] and others have pointed out, that a proposition embodying an hypothesis yields two kinds of consequences. In the first instance are the transformations of a logico-mathematical nature; in the second case are the transformations of an empirical nature. Thus the proposition "The Constitution is the supreme law of the land, and the supreme law of the land must be observed by the Supreme Court" has a number of formal implications, e.g., "The Constitution is the supreme law of the land," "The supreme law of the land must be observed by the Supreme Court" and so on. Formal implications are the life blood of logic and mathematics, but in empirical science our attention is focused upon the implications of the second kind. We want to know the empirical implications of the proposition and not its permissible logical transformations. If the Constitution as it itself declares is the supreme law of the land, then it follows, if we adopt the reasoning of Marshall, Webster, Kent and other expounders of the Constitution, that the Supreme Court is its final interpreter. But the Constitution provides that the United States shall guarantee to every State a republican form of government; nevertheless the Supreme Court has held that it was without jurisdiction to decide whether an initiative and referendum law adopted by the people of Oregon violated this provision. The original hy-

[4] *The Implications of Legal Science* (1933) 10 N. Y. University Law Quarterly Rev. 279, 301.

[5] *Testability and Meaning* (1936) 3 Phil. Sci. Jr. 419, (1937) 4 Phil. Sci. Jr. 1.

pothesis, therefore, that the Constitution is the supreme law of the land, either is erroneous or requires restatement since one of its proper implications is contrary to what actually is the case. If the hypothesis is such that it has no empirical consequences, that is, that its truth or falsity cannot be tested, it carries no interest to science. In such a case it is part of the realm of myth and outside the domain of science.

Transformative rules of an empirical nature are exemplified in physical or biological laws stated as postulates. This presupposes, however, the prior formulation of laws. In the absence of this preliminary formulation, as in the infancy of a science, no general rules exist to guide us in the process of foreseeing empirical consequences. Under these conditions the hypothesis of chromosomes, subjected to formal analysis, would never suggest to us the empirical consequences which would obtain in the organism if chromosomes were present in its cellular structure. In that domain imagination must be our principal guide. In many cases we cannot directly verify an hypothesis and we must then state it in such form that its implications can be tested. No one has ever seen the "Constitution" except as a printed or written document, and the "supreme law of the land" has not been observed in even that form. We can, however, ocularly inspect the nine justices constituting the Supreme Court and observe the operations they conduct. If those operations are in conformity with an implication of the proposition that the Constitution is the supreme law of the land the probability is that the hypothesis is valid. The verification, however, remains only probable since the proposition is intended to cover an infinite number of cases and we are able to make only a finite number of observations. We can never completely verify an empirical hypothesis of this type.

The process of confirmation has two requirements: (a) testability, or the existence of a procedure which permits a confirmation in some degree of the hypothesis; and (b) confirmability, or a knowledge of the conditions under which the hypothesis would be confirmed. An hypothesis can be confirmable but not testable, that is, we may know what conditions would confirm the hypothesis but we are unable to set up the procedure to test it. The hypothesis of absolute time cannot be tested by any known operation, although it would be confirmed by the conditions of Newtonian physics.

CONCEPT AND FACT

Such, in brief, is what is meant by the method of hypothesis and verification. By employing it we hope to acquire knowledge. The basis of this expectation lies in the fact that the utilization of this method by scientists in general has led to knowledge in other fields. The history of science seems to reveal that the method of hypothesis and verification is the universal method of science, applicable alike in such diverse fields as psychology, chemistry, logic and etymology. No reason appears why it is not equally applicable in the field of legal theory.

The outline just presented of the method of hypothesis and verification by no means, however, exhausts the problems which must be considered in any discussion of method in legal science. There are certain questions which, while not peculiar to legal science, it is essential to attempt to answer. At the beginning stand the questions, What is meant by the terms "concept" and "fact"? and, What is the place of concepts in legal theory? A concept may be defined as a word or sign, denoting an abstraction, the meaning of which is dependent upon the determination of its rules of usage.[6] By an abstraction is meant merely the recognition of a form which things have in common apart from any content. So many things in the external world apparently have the same form that we need only a relatively few concepts to collect them in a manageable order. When we abstract the form and symbolize it we have a concept. Thus in law we have the

[6] *Cf.* Campbell, *Physics, The Elements* (1920) 45.

debt created by a judgment; the receipt of money paid by mistake or obtained by fraud; and the privilege to waive a tort and bring an action in contract instead. Looking at these situations and others similar to them, we arrive at the concept of quasi-contract, just as the physicist studying the motions of diverse objects develops the concept of momentum. Legal theory, like most sciences, abounds in concepts. Their practical value is immense. They provide a technical language which generates accuracy and brevity, and conserves energy; they tend to crystallize and maintain what has been learned; and, most important, they may be utilized as instruments of new knowledge. In jurisprudence they have been used improperly so that one branch of the subject itself was assigned the opprobrious name "jurisprudence of conceptions." The mistake lay not in the employment of concepts as such, which is both unavoidable and desirable, but in their improper construction and use. They omitted factors, such as human interests, which a rational system of law could not ignore, and they failed to take account of the necessity of adaptation. Nevertheless, the jurisprudence of conceptions was not without its purpose. It taught us to beware of the tyranny which lurks in an unheeding use of even the most critically constructed concepts.

By the term "fact" [7] is meant whatever is capable of expression in a proposition. It is distinguishable from the proposition which is a statement, true or false, about phenomena; a fact is, it is not true or false; it is that which makes the proposition true or false. It is therefore simply what is the case. For example, to adapt an illustration from Stebbing,[8] that the

---

[7] For an attempt to define a fact as "an empirically verifiable statement about phenomena in terms of a conceptual scheme" see Henderson, *An Approximate Definition of Fact* (1932) 14 Univ. Calif. Pub. in Philos. 179. See also Parsons, *The Structure of Social Action* (1937) 41. For the bases of the view taken here see G. E. Moore, *Facts and Propositions* (1927) Arist. Soc. Sup. Vol. VII, 171.

[8] *A Modern Introduction to Logic* (1930) 36.

Supreme Court is composed of nine justices is the case; that is, it is a fact that the Supreme Court is composed of nine justices. It is this fact that makes the proposition *The Supreme Court is composed of nine justices* true, and that also makes the proposition *The Supreme Court is composed of ten justices* false.

The determination of the place of concepts in legal theory raises some questions of importance. It has been pointed out above that a concept is a word or sign denoting an abstraction. But the mere concepts "law," "tort," "court," "possession," express hardly anything by themselves; they do, however, suggest to the mind a reference to a situation which obtains in the external world which is more or less familiar. This reference is vague, non-assertive and of rudimentary utility. It is only when we employ the word or sign in a proposition or sentence that we enter or approach the realm of fact. When we say, "The transfer of possession is one of the chief methods of transferring ownership," we are making an assertion about the concept of possession which can be verified or disproved. Now we can make two kinds of assertions about legal concepts. We may make an assertion which is formally true, *i.e.*, deducible logically from an antecedent proposition, or we may utter an assertion which is susceptible of verification or disproof. All other assertions, to borrow the language of the logical positivists, are strictly nonsensical or pseudo-propositions. Montesquieu's assertion that "Law in general is human reason" is a pseudo-proposition unless we are able to devise some technique to test its truth or falsity. If we knew what analyses would lead us to accept or reject it, then we could say that Montesquieu was not talking nonsense but had said something significant. Propositions therefore which are not merely formally true, and which are significant, are in reality hypotheses. Thus they should conform to all the requirements of genuine hypotheses, one of which is that an hypothesis should be capable of verification.

A concept then is an instrument which permits us to obtain

new knowledge. We translate it into a genuine hypothesis which we verify or disprove. The hypothesis itself is to some degree a summary of our past experience and at the same time an anticipation of future occurrences. If the hypothesis is verified the concept, in accordance with the assertion made in the proposition, has a legitimate place in the legal structure. It becomes a source of new knowledge as the premise for formal deductions. Unfortunately, in spite of the vast amount of analysis which has been devoted to them, legal concepts, from the point of view of a general theory of law, require almost complete restatement. No really satisfactory statement can perhaps be achieved until comparative law is much further advanced than it is at present. Even then, when we will be able to formulate hypotheses of complete general-' ity, the task will be only half accomplished. All the propositions elucidating the concepts will have to be restated in terms of a normative science, which itself has still to be born. In this field, however, the immediate task of a general theory of law is large enough to occupy our energies for many years to come. We possess enough knowledge to frame sentences of sufficient factual significance to permit at least a beginning. The new knowledge of the future will allow a greater clarification and the establishment of relations between concepts in the interests of wider systematization.

THE LEGAL PROPOSITION AND LEGAL SCIENCE

Legal science, to the exclusion of nearly all other considerations, has devoted itself in the past to the study of the legal proposition. It has been the essential subject matter of legal speculation from antiquity to the present day. It has, however, been studied from a point of view entirely different from that suggested here.

As the subject matter of nearly all legal science, legal propositions have been regarded not as empirical hypotheses, but as precepts. That is, they are taken to be rules or norms prescribing a course of conduct. As such, they have been exhaustively analyzed. Generations of scholars have devoted themselves to the study of their origins, to their elucidation and clarification, to the development of techniques for their proper formulation, even quite appropriately to the metaphysical problem of whether the legal proposition exists merely as a form of words or in some other more realistic sense. These are all legitimate tasks for men intent upon making a particular legal system function properly. How far that task is still short of accomplishment we realize when we reflect that none of the problems which the legal scholars have undertaken to investigate has been solved. This is not necessarily due to the fact, as seems to be the case with metaphysicians, that legal scholars have been asking themselves questions inherently incapable of an answer; rather, it may be a consequence of the enormous complexity of the material which legal scholars are attempting to analyze. Some questions, however, which legal scholars have propounded have been strictly nonsensical, that is, they are inherently incapable of being answered, e.g.: What principle does a particular case decide? Since, as Oliphant has shown, numerous principles can be suggested as the basis of any particular decision, it is nonsensical to assert that any particular case decides a principle as its *ratio decidendi*. The labor and devotion which jurists have given to studies of this order have added immeasurably to our knowledge of the workings of legal systems. They have, however, with exceptions here and there, been intent upon the legal proposition as a legal precept. That is a sound enough view for a technology of law. It is inadequate, however, for a general theory of law.

The proposition of a general theory of law is, as was shown above, either a formally true proposition or an empirical hypothesis. It is not in any sense a precept, although one of the empirical hypotheses of such a general theory may well be a proposition of the kind: "The legal propositions of established systems of law are precepts." This does not mean that the tasks to which jurists have given their attention in the past are to be excluded from consideration in the formulation of a general theory of law. They are part of the subject matter of a general theory in the sense that the conduct of the jurists in relation to the tasks illuminates and accounts for the structure of the system of law prevailing in a particular area.

Legal science must thus depend, at the outset at all events, upon the method of hypothesis and verification. It is not suggested that this method be employed to the exclusion of all others. As particular problems are encountered, the comparative, the statistical and other methods will no doubt contribute materially to their solution. The ideal of legal science, however, will always be in the direction of a validly constructed postulational system, the postulates of which will be empirical hypotheses. This suggestion explicitly recognizes the importance in their formulation of the role of logic, philosophy, and ethics. It recognizes, in brief, the legitimacy of any of the tools which men have found trustworthy in arriving at knowledge.

7.

THE FIELD OF INVESTIGATION

AMONG THE ANCIENT ASSYRIANS the priests who were entrusted with the task of exorcizing demons had above everything else to discover the particular kind of demon with whom they had to deal. Frequently, however, knowledge of the demon's name was not attainable, and then recourse was had to the recital of the name of every possible kind of demon. Social theorists are very much in the position of the ancient Assyrian priests. No revelation of their subject matter has been vouchsafed to them; their most prudent course would appear to consider as their own the widest possible field of inquiry.

THE NATURE OF THE PROBLEM

At the heart of social inquiry is the problem of social change. It is also, since jurisprudence is a branch of social inquiry, inescapably at the center of juristic thinking. English law has an unbroken history of fifteen hundred years. It is today vastly different from what it was at its inception, or at the time of the Norman Conquest, or in Blackstone's period, or at the beginning of the Twentieth Century. American law has had a much shorter period of continuous development, but it also has undergone similar transformations. It is something very much different today from what it was such a short time ago as the year 1932, before the courts had passed upon the cases engendered by the legislation and activities arising from the economic depression of 1929. American law, in greater or less respect, will certainly in ten years, a hundred years, a thousand years, be again something unlike what we know today. Why do those transformations occur? How do those modifications take place? In the process of invention, growth, accommodation, decay, renewal, and disappearance, are there any principles discernible? These are some of the questions which a general theory of law must consider. Any theory which does not take account of them is fatally incomplete. It ignores perhaps the most significant characteristic of social life.

The effort to isolate or understand the principles of change is also the first step towards the delimitation of the field of inquiry. At the outset it was stated provisionally that the subject matter of jurisprudence is the study of human behavior as a function of disorder. It has been shown that there are many systems of order in society which require many kinds of conduct on the part of the members, and that there is disorder when behavior does not conform to the demands of the relations established by the systems. Valid inquiry insists, however, that the subject matter be further delimited, so that out of the almost overwhelmingly complex material which is observable there can be selected the data which are relevant. All the systems of order of which society is comprised may bear upon the kinds of human behavior with which jurisprudence is concerned; but at the outset, at any rate, if we are not to be inundated in confusion, it is the sounder method to choose those which appear immediately material. If we seek for the principles of change applicable to the legal order, we are at the same time circumscribing the area of systems of order material to legal inquiry. Such an undertaking focuses our attention upon the systems of order which contribute to the phenomenon of legal change. It assumes that legal change is a resultant of the functioning of systems of order demanding particular kinds of behavior.

This view does not overlook the possibility of the discovery of permanent elements existent in legal systems. It would at this stage of the inquiry, however, be premature to attempt to characterize those elements, if they exist. They may be products, forms or relations, and any effort to define them would be arbitrary, relating to nothing known to us in the external world. Moreover, since observation and analysis have not revealed any such elements to us in the past, it seems probable that a future demarcation will of necessity be arbitrary. It will be a demarcation undertaken for the purposes of systematization, coherence and generality, and will correspond only approximately to the facts of perceptual experience. Thus, the delimitation of any such elements will be an abstraction, and an abstraction, as Whitehead has remarked, "is nothing else than omission of part of the truth." Nevertheless, an end product of scientific inquiry is always abstraction; and the isolation of the permanent, though it belong to the world of the abstract, is a task which cannot be avoided.

THE CHARACTER OF CHANGE

Change is a complex notion and its meaning is far from clear. In the vivid mythology of the Greeks, Chronos was thought of as a being who begat children and himself devoured them. They conceived of the world as one of constant change, a world "of coming into being and passing away." This was the view of Heraclitus in the Sixth Century B.C. Change is the only reality, it is constant and everlasting, πάντα ῥεῖ. This is Bergson's doctrine today. It is scarcely necessary to add that from the time of Parmenides and Zeno to that of Spinoza and F. H. Bradley, the notion has, seriously or paradoxically, been fervently combatted.

Moreover, the arguments against the idea of a changing thing seem irrefutable. When we say that a thing changes we assert that A, which existed yesterday, is today A^1 and tomorrow will be A^2. If, however, A does not in some sense persist into the states A^1 and A^2 we have no basis to assert that

A[1] yesterday was A. We must be able to find some identity
between A and A[1] in order to assert that A[1] yesterday was A.
We obviously cannot do that if change operates in the whole
of A. If it does not, some element of A is permanent, which
is what those who deny the reality of change assert. We thus
come to the present-day view that change consists either of
the alteration of position of permanent entities or the reality
of, if change is insisted upon, the creation and destruction of
impermanent entities. In this latter view, which has support
in quantum theory, a man is not a continuous organism but a
series of organisms annihilated and generated with a frequency
in proportion to the length of the time interval necessary for
the change to operate.[1] It is recognized that such conclusions
will hardly satisfy anyone, and that they are scarcely more
than a shadow of the truth, if that. The problem is, however,
as Broad has remarked, "the hardest knot in the whole of
philosophy." We may leave the metaphysical perplexities of
change at that point and see if we are able to ascribe a working content to the concept.

Our problem is the reconciliation of identity and difference. When we say that an object has changed, there must
remain in the changed object enough identity for us to assert
that we are contemplating the same object, in spite of the
changes. Notwithstanding the laws of logic we are able to
make this assertion. A cabinet-maker manipulates a pile of lumber and a desk appears. The lumber has certainly disappeared
and a desk has come into being. Nevertheless, we assert that it
is the same wood. Those who say that the world consists of non-
enduring units, or in other words, that change is universal,
deny that it is the same wood, since the wood itself has been
undergoing change in all its essential properties. This follows
quite correctly from the premises and may in fact be the case.
Our ordinary sense perceptions, however, recognize sufficient

---

[1] Bradley, *Appearance and Reality* (1920) c. v; Bergson, *La Perception du Changement* (1911); Lewis, *Mind and the World Order* (1929)
396 *et seq.*

identity between the wood in the desk and the wood in the pile of lumber for us to say that it is the same wood. If change is universal it is not the same wood, and our assertion that it is rests merely upon the basis that our instruments are too crude to detect the changes which have taken place. That, however, is the fact; we do not perceive the change in the series of time intervals within which we operate. If the wood is burned, leaving ashes, we are then able to perceive that the wood has changed. To rest our identification upon the crudity of our instruments is unsatisfactory and dangerous, since our instruments may some day be perfected. That, however, belongs to the world of tomorrow; today we make the identification in spite of logical rules and it is within the framework of such experience that we must determine the meaning of change.

Change is an ambiguous term and is used in a number of senses.[2] The most important are:

1. Change in the attributes of things, as where a traffic light changes from red to green.

2. Change of place of a thing by motion, as where the hands of a clock change from ten A.M. to eleven A.M.

3. The conclusion of an event or cessation of a continued existence of some kind. That is what happens when an object ceases to be present, becomes past, and is not recoverable in perception, but only in memory. Examples are the conclusion of opinion day in the Supreme Court and the reduction of wood to ashes.

4. The occurrence of a new event, as when the Securities and Exchange Commission was created by Act of Congress.

Such are the principal meanings we employ when we use a sentence with the word change in it. No useful purpose would be achieved if we attempted to combine these mean-

2 Broad, *Scientific Thought* (1936) 67; Gunn, *The Problem of Time* (1930) 292.

ings into one definition. Eubank [3] has formulated a careful
and inclusive sociological definition which does in fact accomplish such an objective but which at the same time fails
to emphasize the radically different meanings of the term.
Change, he writes, is "any alteration that occurs in (1) the
position or (2) the condition of anything from a state previously existent." It should be noted that the various meanings
of change are equally applicable to cultural and social change.
There is a widely held view that the direct concern of sociologists is with social relationships, and that social change
is a different thing from cultural change, entering in a different way into the time process. The latter conclusion follows
from the fact that culture is represented by products which
persist, or change slowly, and thus by their presence exert a
continuous influence, while the society in which they are present lives on only as a changing equilibrium of present relationships.[4] Such a distinction may have importance for the
purposes of formal sociology but it is here unnecessary. Our
immediate attention is directed to the systems of order requir-
ing particular kinds of behavior and the manner in which they
contribute to the phenomenon of legal change. Those systems
of order are functions of both cultural products and social
relationships. To omit one or the other is to ignore half the
picture.

LEGAL THEORIES OF CHANGE

In legal theory the problem of legal flux is treated much
more narrowly than in social theory. It is generally examined
under the topic "sources of the law," a phrase which jurists
themselves recognize to be markedly ambiguous. Its three
principal meanings are: (1) the source which gives legal
precepts their authority; (2) the agencies to which legal precepts owe their existence; and (3) the authoritative reposi-
tories of legal precepts to which courts refer for guidance. We

[3] *The Concepts of Sociology* (1932) 261.
[4] MacIver, *Society* (1931) 392.

are concerned here with the use of the phrase in its second meaning.

It is unnecessary at this stage of the inquiry to enter into the juridical controversy over the manner in which legal rules arise. For the purposes of Anglo-American jurisprudence the problem has been correctly envisaged and is a real one. The Anglo-American jurist has been concerned with the question: What are the immediate sources of law? To this question various answers have been proposed and elaborately defended. The answers have included, as among the sources, custom, judicial precedents, legislation, opinions of experts, principles of morality, usage, and equity. Some writers accept them all, others in the interest of precision and certainty select only a few. Maine [5] thought that law was "brought into harmony with society" through the instrumentality of "Legal Fictions, Equity, and Legislation." He went further and attempted to establish an historical sequence for them, asserting that he knew "of no instance in which the order of their appearance has been changed or inverted." Holdsworth,[6] however, insists that Maine's generalization "will not fit the facts of English history." It has been argued that the whole controversy is ultimately meaningless and unreal on the ground that the sources lie elsewhere. Nevertheless, the Anglo-American jurist has had his eye upon an important and tangible reality. The sources which have been enumerated are the sources to which the judge turns in deciding controversies. The interests of an adequate jurisprudence demand that we have an accurate and as precisely a delimited enumeration of such sources as it is possible to obtain. They are the sources to which the judge turns immediately in the decision of controversies; and since that function is his principal one, a theory of law must take full account of it.

However, a wider view is required here in the interests of generality. The function of a general theory of law is not to

[5] *Ancient Law* (World's Classics ed.) 20.
[6] *Sources and Literature of English Law* (1925) 2.

discover the immediate sources of law, however important that may be in the study of a particular area, but to segregate the factors which operate in all areas in the creation, modification, transformation and disappearance of legal systems. The sources of law as they have been isolated by Anglo-American jurists simply will not fit the facts of Continental law, Roman law, archaic and primitive law and other systems. Procrustean subtleties may give the appearance of generality, but it is at the sacrifice of logic, history and reality. Sources agreed upon for one period of legal history are not the sources even at a different period of what we are accustomed to treat as the same system. In Roman law, the sources were one thing during the republic, a different thing during the principiate, and yet a different thing during the dominate. They were one thing in American law during the Nineteenth Century and they are another thing today. We cannot dismiss as naïve speculation the ideas which other peoples have of the sources of their own law. In the Institutes of Manu four sources are enumerated: Revelation, or the uttered thoughts of inspired seers; the institutes of revered sages, handed down by word of mouth from generation to generation; the approved and immemorial usages of the people; and that which satisfies the sense of equity, and is acceptable to reason.[7] Sources such as those, including our own, are relative to time and the existing culture; they are a function of the particular civilization in which they obtain.

A general theory of law, however, must search for the enduring circumstances of change, the permanent conditions present in all cultures. It must emphasize not the diversities of culture, but the basic unities of the social process. These unities have been firmly established by modern critical anthropology and sociology. The astonishing unities which studies in those fields have disclosed are of more significance than the differences in matters of detail which have also been

[7] Holland, *Jurisprudence* (10th ed. 1906) 54 n. 1.

revealed. The unity of history, in the sense of a similarity of social structure and perhaps of tendencies, provides a solid basis for generalization and the construction of a general scientific theory. Accordingly, the first task of a science of law, when confronted with the problem of legal change, is to isolate the factors which make for change in all cultures, to discover how and what they contribute, and whether there is any ascertainable direction in the constant ebb and flow of social processes.

THE TASK OF CLASSIFICATION

At its present stage jurisprudence, together with economics, biology, psychology, geography and many other subjects, is predominantly a descriptive science. That is to say, the energies of workers in the field of jurisprudence must for the most part be expended in the collection of data, and in their classification, correlation, and symbolization. In this activity conjectures and hypotheses are the signposts which direct the observer to the data which may be relevant. The observer operates primarily in the realm of the brute fact. Every fact that he discovers might, for all he knows, or has the right to expect, have been entirely different. If in one area cases are decided in accordance with rules promulgated by a body of men called legislators, he is not surprised if in the next area they are decided in accordance with principles of right and justice located in the head of the judge. He may expect no triumphs of the kind which mark the development of the exact sciences. Sir William Hamilton's mathematical prediction of the existence of conical refraction, which had never been observed, but which was verified experimentally a year later, is a feat which he can hardly hope to emulate. Nor is he much interested, at this period of his inquiry, at any rate, in explanation. He is more concerned with ascertaining how the processes he observes operate than in why they operate. As jurisprudence begins to take on more of the characteristics of the exact sciences, as its propositions become systematized and integrated, the latter question is one which must be taken account of in order to complete the inquiry; but at the beginning it is not in the immediate foreground. Our present task is the delimitation of the field of inquiry. "The ordering of facts and their relationships in each individual science," Ostwald has written, "is the first and most important function in its development." Classification is the primary technique which has been created to accomplish this end. It should be observed, however, that the data we look for, and the way we classify them, will be circumscribed by two barriers. We will in the first place look only for such facts as are relevant and crucial; and what appears relevant and crucial will be determined by our initial ideas and by the elements of the problem we are undertaking to solve. In the second place, we are prisoners of the condition of our particular culture. As Dewey has insisted, if we look at earlier times, it is clear that certain problems could not have arisen in the cultural pattern that then existed, and that if, *per impossible,* they had been capable of detection and formulation, there were no means available for solving them. "There is an inalienable and ineradicable framework of conceptions which is not of our own making, but given to us ready-made by society," Cornford [8] has written, "—a whole apparatus of concepts and categories within which and by which individual thinking, however daring and original, is compelled to move." No doubt, we would, if we were wise, like philosophy, exclude nothing from our classification scheme. Such a procedure, however, would not only be self-defeating, it would be impossible of accomplishment. "All classification," Whitehead [9] has pointed out, "depends on the current character of importance."

We classify in order to organize our knowledge and in the hope that it will shed some light on our understanding of the nature of things. The importance of the idea of organization

[8] *From Religion to Philosophy* (1912) 45, quoted by Stebbing, *A Modern Introduction to Logic* (1930) 16 n. 1.
[9] *Modes of Thought* (1938) 21-22.

was insisted upon in ancient times by Aristotle, and its significance for modern thought has been affirmed in a classic
essay by L. J. Henderson. "I believe," he [10] writes, "that organization has finally become a category which stands beside
those of matter and energy . . . The fact is that for science
the idea of organization . . . is today a component part of the
theoretical description of nature." In a descriptive science
such as jurisprudence the organization achieved by classification is far below the level contemplated by Henderson, if indeed it is not something entirely different. At the beginning it
can represent no more than an effort to systematize the field
of inquiry, group together the data which exhibit similarities
and above all to serve as a definitive map of the area to be
explored so that no relevant data will be overlooked and all
the relevant data will be included. Classification in a descriptive science is the preparation of an agendum of operations.
Jevons' [11] view that "the purpose of classification is the detection of the laws of nature" may be sound enough at the higher
levels of science; but at the level of a rudimentary descriptive
science it is inapplicable. When chemists select from the list
of metals, because of their analogous properties, potassium,
sodium, cesium, rubidium, and lithium, and call them the
alkaline metals, it may be expected that a discovery of properties in one of the metals will also be exhibited by the remaining four. In jurisprudence our knowledge is yet so un-
developed that we cannot hope to operate in this manner.
Any hidden resemblances which resulted from a classification
would be, so far as we have the right to anticipate, entirely
fortuitous. This is so because our purpose of classification is
different. We are merely charting the area in which we intend to function, and are grouping, from the point of view of
coherence and utility, the elements to which we intend to give
particular attention.

[10] *The Order of Nature* (1925) 67.
[11] *The Principles of Science* (1892) 675.

Classification is essentially a mental operation.[12] It is not an operation on an event but a method of thinking about an event. When we classify we apply a word to a group of events which have a certain character. Thus, a "class" is a group of all the events and only those to which a particular concept is applicable. Classes, as Whitehead and Russell point out,[13] are "merely symbolic or linguistic conveniences, not genuine objects as their members are if they are individuals." Classes are constructed in one of two ways. We either enumerate a group, such as mammals, birds, reptiles, amphibians and fishes, and search for a word which will describe a common characteristic, in this case, "vertebrate"; or, we reverse the process, and start with the word "vertebrate," applying it to all objects having the characteristic of a vertebra.

THE ELEMENTS OF THE LEGAL STRUCTURE

If the task of jurisprudence is the study of human behavior as a function of disorder, it follows that all behavior which may be seen in this relationship is within the field of legal inquiry. In its broadest aspect all behavior may probably on analysis be shown to be within the scope of this concept. It is necessary, therefore, to bring the inquiry within manageable limits; otherwise we are defeated at the threshold. There would be no end to an investigation of every variety and kind of conduct. We must therefore devise a criterion which will permit us to narrow the field of operations in order to eliminate what appears unimportant and at the same time direct our attention to what seems relevant and crucial.

At the initiation of the inquiry the most useful criterion appears to be the isolation of the elements or constants which in all areas in which relatively homogeneous systems of law prevail are directly within the domain of legal operations.

[12] Bliss, *The Organization of Knowledge* (1929) 144; Benjamin, *Philosophy of Science* (1937) 121.

[13] *Principia Mathematica* (1st ed. 1910) 75.

There seem to be six such elements present in all known systems of law, whether modern, ancient or archaic, or primitive. First, there are the regulations of behavior with respect to persons. In a broad sense this is the fundamental category, and all other elements are subdivisions of it. It should be remembered, however, that we are classifying only for purposes of description and not explanation. We are directing attention to the universal behavior elements which everywhere and at all times have been the concern of the law. Why that is the case, and what their relationship is to one another must await the outcome of the first inquiry. Under this topic would be studied the liabilities of individuals for their conduct, and their powers to affect the conduct of others. That is a large field, and embraces both tort and crime without attempting to distinguish between them, inasmuch as any such distinction would be merely a lawyer's convention limited in area and possessing few consequences of general social importance. Although it is an extensive field, it is not one beyond the range of description, provided it is attacked systematically. It is impossible, however, to outline one system suitable for all areas. That was the vitiating error of the work of the earlier comparative ethnologists. In the sociology of religion, for example, to attempt to fit all religious conduct into the framework of preconceived notions of sect, denomination, cult and ecclesia could result only in a description that was basically false. Each area must be studied in its own terms and in accordance with the order-relationships which prevail in it. Such studies will yield descriptions of the behavior capabilities and powers of the individuals within the areas; they will disclose the systems constructed within those areas to control behavior in the relations of disorder there prevailing. Above all, if we systematize only in terms of the area to be described and do not attempt a specious generality at the outset, we are more likely to include what is essential. Until the results of a sufficient number of area investigations are before us, it would be risky to pronounce on what was significant and what was not. Among the Wanika of Eastern Africa, for example, "if a man dares to improve the style of his hut, to make a larger doorway than is customary . . . he is instantly fined." [14] Such an example of behavior Westermarck [15] felt was too detailed for students of customs in their generality. What is it that entitles us, however, to pronounce such a verdict in the absence of full descriptions of behavior from many areas analyzed from the point of view of the frameworks of the particular areas and from that of the structure of society in general? For the legal student, thinking of the system of behavior established by modern zoning ordinances, the fact that a people of rudimentary culture have established a similar system may be of great significance.

A second element is the associations or groups of persons whose collective behavior is subject to legal regulation. An association, as the term is here employed, means any group of persons who maintain social relationships with each other and whose behavior as a group is subject to legal control. It includes the family, the church, the trade association, the partnership and the corporation, the secret society of primitive and modern cultures, the kinship group and so on. Associations in one form or another are common features of all areas and their conduct has consequences of a legal kind which fall into an easily recognized category. From the association we pass to the third element, the community, which embraces the common life of a definite area. It includes the tribe and the village, the county and the country, the city and the nation. All communities have some sort of organization, some locus of authority, some arrangement for its exercise. The organization may be, as among the desperate peoples of Beagle Channel, of a most rudimentary kind; it may be, as in America, complex, sophisticated and elaborately supervised. The behavior of communities is also a matter of legal concern.

[14] New, *Life in Eastern Africa* (1874) 110.
[15] 1 *Origin and Development of the Moral Ideas* (1912) 327.

The authority of the community is canalized within patterns of a legal kind, and such patterns comprise its constitution. We must not press the notion of a constitution beyond its legitimate limits and seek to identify in all areas features which may very well be absent. A brief description of the community organization of a rudimentary people may exhaust all that is properly conceived of as constitutional in that system. Although it is a universal element of the legal order, it may not possess real significance at all levels.

We pass now from persons and aggregates of persons to two institutions which are everywhere a feature of human culture and which are elements in all legal structures—property and promises. There is a tendency in sociology today to treat contract as an aspect of property and such a conception of the organization of property has undoubted uses. In most, if not all, systems of law, however, the two concepts are clearly distinguishable and are given separate treatment. In the interests of clarity it seems advisable at the outset to follow that practice and to study the behavior relationships of each separately. They are the major focal points of the institutional activity of law in all areas. The controls which have been constructed regulating activity in relation to them are multitudinous, and permeate the legal structure in all its interstices. If full descriptions of the legal regulation of human conduct with respect to property and promises are obtained, the structure of the law is largely exhausted. Like the notion of person, those two concepts have been basic in most legal thinking and activity.

Administration, or the system through which the law of a community is maintained, is the sixth and last element. Under it would be described the kinds of sanctions, the forms of procedure, the jurisdiction of courts if any, ceremonialism, and other methods devised to insure orderly responses to the behavior patterns established with respect to the preceding five elements. Administration is also a universal feature of social life, although in many areas it has achieved only a rudimentary development.

It should be said at once that the six elements enumerated above must be regarded as tentative. Other methods of attaining the desired end will appeal to different students. To a follower of Le Play it will seem preferable to select some single unit, comparable (say) to the cell in biology, the study of which will yield all that we desire to know. Such a unit is difficult to find in law, although if the court is taken as the unit it comes close to meeting the requirements and possesses the additional advantage that it can be quantitatively studied. Nevertheless, the proposed method seems as likely as any to lead us to the objectives we have in mind. It meets the essential requirement that it can be so handled that it will satisfy the logical conditions of a valid method.

Our immediate objective is a reasonably full description of the legal structures which prevail and have prevailed in the different socially homogeneous areas of the earth. Such descriptions are the essential starting points for a genuine comparative method. Unlike the physical scientist, the social scientist must assume an ultimate disorder which, through various means, has been fashioned into an order characteristic of the features of the area in which it obtains. The physical scientist may assume that the characteristics of a hydrogen atom will be the same wherever he encounters it. But the social scientist has not yet isolated such units. All the units upon which he operates and regards as similar are but rough approximations of one another. Insofar as his researches have progressed, the orders required by those units vary from area to area. Until he has full knowledge of the orders of each area he is unable to state whether or not there is something which may be described as a general order. We have learned also from the mistakes of the past that we cannot study the form of conduct, the idea, or the interest as isolated units. They must be studied, if we are not to go astray, in the social setting of the society in which they exist; otherwise we are more than likely to attribute our own presuppositions to them.

If we are fortunate enough to obtain such descriptions we are then able to compare the orders of one area with those of another. That comparison will yield propositions of general applicability, and serve as the basis to take us into the explanatory realm, or it will not. If the latter alternative turns out to be the case, we will then have learned that the order of each area is unique and that the data of other areas cannot help to explain it. Such an eventuality seems unlikely in view of the extensive contacts between cultures; but it is a possibility which we should always bear in mind. If we find that we are able to construct general propositions in accordance with a method which is logically satisfactory, the way has been opened for a general science of law.

Such a step forward, however, is only one part of the picture. The orders of any area are not constants, but moving equilibriums in a constant condition of flux. What are the factors which are responsible for the appearance of the six elements we have enumerated in all known legal systems? Why is the condition of these elements impermanent and in what, if any, direction is there movement? These are questions the importance of which has already been indicated. They will be considered in detail in the following chapter.

8.

THE NATURE OF LEGAL CHANGE

IT IS CONVENIENT, as we have seen, to isolate from the structures of the known legal systems the elements common to all. There appear to be six such elements: the regulations of behavior with respect to persons, associations, property and promises, the constitution of the community and the sustaining administrative system. Like all that comprises the external world, these elements in their aspects at least are impermanent; their characteristics are not today what they were yesterday. It has been an endless task to present an intelligible account of this phenomenon, and the clarification of the problem is one of the necessities of present-day thought.

ACTIVITY AND RELATIONS

Change appears to be a complex of two distinct notions, activity and relationship. This has long been recognized in metaphysics; but it is only in modern times that these ideas have been carefully explored in social theory. At present, particularly in France and Germany, they are utilized as the basis of far-reaching systems, and writers such as Brunhes, anxious to purge their subjects of non-rigorous elements, take them as the sole point of departure. There is little question of the indispensable importance of the notions of activity and relation; but a satisfactory definition of them seems impossible, since any definition would contain terms equally basic and thus equally in need of definition. Both concepts were fundamental in Aristotle's terminology and the first, activity, has its roots in animistic thought, *e.g.*, the observable action of water upon physical things, and the nature of volition. Lotze thought that the notion of activity was unanalyzable and Bradley rejected both the idea of activity and of relationship as indefensible and nonsensical. His arguments are held generally to be unsound, however, although a refutation of his celebrated argument against relations would be a difficult technical achievement, and has perhaps never been fully attempted. In physics action is defined simply as energy multiplied by time. This notion, however, has no place in social thought, since there is no place for any precise notion of energy.

It is perhaps most helpful to define activity as behavior or movement of any kind and wherever found. If a more definite idea is desired with respect to the activity of human beings, the psychological conception of any muscular or glandular change which results from motor nerve impulse seems adequate enough. A relation may be taken to mean the way one thing is connected or "has to do" with another. Naked activity is unintelligible in the absence of the notion of relationship, since activity can be understood or measurable only in relationship to some other thing. We may therefore define change as the appearance of a new relationship.

We are, however, only at the threshold of our problem. There are many types of activities and many types of relationships. We stand in need of a criterion which will indicate the significant in the web of activities and relationships which confronts us. At the outset we are faced with alternative methods of approach. We may ask: Why did a particular change occur? Or we may ask: How did a particular change occur? The first question is causal and it is more than doubtful that it can be made to possess any significance. We may venture answers to it but then verification will always remain conjectural. Causality has had an unhappy time in the history of science and has muddied the waters of social theory perhaps more than any other notion. We have developed no sound technique for handling it, even assuming that we know what it means, and its complete abandonment would remove one of the major sources of error in our thinking. Its effect upon modern thought is as unfortunate as the consequences of the notion of place upon dynamics prior to Galileo. The Aristotelians of his day explained the descent of heavy bodies and the ascent of light bodies (as in liquids) upon the theory that every body had its place. Below was the place of heavy bodies; above, that of light bodies. Moreover, the notion of cause is unnecessary. An alternative approach will yield for the present, at any rate, all the knowledge we are able to digest.

If we inquire: How did a particular change occur? we pass into the realms of history and system. We are asking a question which is intelligible to scientists generally and the answer to which has at least the possibility of verification. In most cases we would know what observations to conduct in order to accept the answer as true or to reject it as false. More important, however, this approach yields the criterion for which we are seeking. We ask: What is the system of relations which confronts us? What is the activity which occurs in that system? If there is a change in the system we ask: What is the change in the system? What is the change, if any, in the activity? If we know the answers to these questions we have gone a long way towards the establishment of a science of law. We have focused upon that which is essential in the construction of such a system.

THE DESCRIPTION OF ACTIVITY

It will simplify our task if we consider the second question first: What is the activity which occurs in the system of relationships we designate as legal? The precise problem is to

determine whether or not our inquiry is exhausted when we have
defined activity as behavior or movement. There are four
ways of looking at behavior as it manifests itself in society in
general and in the system of legal relationships in particular.
We may consider merely behavior itself, regarding it simply
as an activity which has occurred or is occurring; we may
think of it as continuous change; we may consider it as having a direction in time or as taking place in a definite manner; or we may view it in some combination of the foregoing.

All the ways of looking at behavior present serious difficulties,
but some form of the first seems most free from error. If our
attention, at the outset at any rate, is focused upon behavior
per se, if our inquiry is to determine what occurs when we
are in the presence of activity, we have made at least a good
start. Mere description, if it is neither the beginning nor the
end of wisdom, is certainly a part of it. We want to know
with as much precision as possible how people behaved under
the systems of legal relations of which we have knowledge.
The pitfalls of such an undertaking are obvious. We must first
isolate with much arbitrariness what we choose to regard as a
system of legal relationships. Is the common law one system
or a name for a multiplicity of systems? If we mean by the
common law the substantive rules which have obtained since
the time of Edward I then plainly we cannot regard it as one
system. We use the same labels for substantive notions that
Blackstone and Kent employed but we mean by them something entirely different. If, however, we search for a fundamental idea which has persisted since the time of what we
choose to regard as the origin of the common law, we may be
successful in devising it. We have before us, though, the example of Holmes, who in spite of a bent towards generalization made no effort to isolate a basic notion underlying the
whole of the common law. We should not, however, lay too
much stress upon this example, which may be accounted for
upon other grounds, particularly in view of the fruitful insight which has resulted from attempts at generalization in

the past. Moreover, even if we regard so vast a system as the common law as a unity, we have not overcome the vice of what Croce [1] terms periodization. Is there a real line of demarcation between Anglo-Saxon law and the law that begins with Edward I? Such divisions are ideal and rarely correspond to abrupt pauses in the life of mankind. They are convenient methods of classification and as such are useful, although we should be careful not to permit them to lead us into error. It is probable that we cannot escape from them; they are too much a part of our mental outlook. The periodization of the past into antiquity, the Middle Ages and modern times is a way of regarding what has occurred from which no present-day mind can entirely hope to free itself.

We must not think that the mere observation of behavior as it takes place in a legal system is the entire task. Such a view is at the root of the mistaken notion that the accumulation of facts will by itself lead us to statements of generality. As Jevons [2] has observed, this notion represents a kind of scientific bookkeeping. Facts are to be indiscriminately gathered from every source, and posted in a ledger, from which will emerge in time a balance of truth. Nothing is less likely to happen. We must approach behavior in its setting of legal relationships with an initial hypothesis, constructed perhaps at first with reference to a particular system, of what is significant. It is easy and impressive to ask large questions, but as the history of philosophical speculation shows, they are rarely answered. In the social sciences, as in the natural sciences, we are much more likely to receive responses to small questions. What promises were enforced in the courts of Edward I and how? is a question to which we may reasonably expect an answer; and, coupling it with other information, we may arrive at a fairly accurate view of a small field of behavior at that time. What is the origin of contract? is a large question;

[1] History, Its Theory and Practice (1921) 112.
[2] The Principles of Science (1892) 576.

but we possess no technique which will permit us to bring an answer to that question to a conclusive test. We must, above all, as many jurists have done, avoid, so far as may be, thinking of the behavior of a system as a state or condition. We must recognize freely the ideal nature of any system we describe and never cease our efforts to increase its correspondence with the ever changing world it purports to represent.

To think of behavior as involving continuous change, while this perhaps is closer to the truth than to regard it as an activity which has occurred or is occurring, takes us beyond the range of techniques now available. If everything changes then we cannot tell what it is that changes. In such a world, as Kant observed, only the permanent can change. But the determination of the permanent and the impermanent involves too hazardous an undertaking and one which is not necessary.

If we think of activity as a process, we think of it as having a direction in time or as taking place in a definite manner or both. At this point we pass from the realm of the neutral. In its most common usage in social thought the notion has been best defined by Small: [3] "A process is a collection of occurrences, each of which has a meaning for every other, the whole of which constitutes some sort of becoming." It is a short step from this conception to the effort to determine the sort of "becoming" which takes place. "Evolution," "progress," "growth," "development" are some of the terms employed to give a precise content to "becoming." Long prior to Savigny, who has been termed a Darwinian before Darwin, and continuing to the present day, these notions have deeply influenced juristic thought. Maine insisted that "even jurisprudence itself cannot escape from that great law of evolution." Nevertheless, the notions remain nothing more than dogmas. In its most prevalent form "becoming" is thought of as a movement from the simple to the complex, but we at once encounter the difficulty that we are without any criteria to determine what

[3] *General Sociology* (1905) 513.

is "simple" and what is "complex." Cohen [4] has pertinently in-
quired if the evolution of the horse's hoof from four toes is a
movement from the simple to the complex. Similarly, shall we
say that the complete abrogation of an entire field of the law,
such as the law of slavery, is a development of the law from
the simple to the complex? We can undoubtedly find many
examples in legal history which give the appearance of a
transition from simplicity to complexity, but we cannot say
that the process is universal as long as facts exist which con-
tradict it. The employment of such terms as "growth" and
"development" represents an effort to escape from what are
conceived to be the unfashionable implications of evolutionary
dogma, but they embrace equally impossible positions. A
developmental series possesses a direction in time; it represents an unfolding of qualities actually or potentially present
in all members of the series, and exhibits the attainment of a
definite result.[5] This notion has been long abandoned by biol-
ogists and is employed today only as an imaginative figure of
speech. For all our present knowledge tells us, Bateson's in-
version of the idea may be just as valid. He suggested that
evolution has taken place through the steady loss of inhibiting
factors. Living matter was stopped down, so to speak, at the
beginning of the world. As the stops are lost new things
emerge. The germinal material has changed only in that it
has become simpler.[6] Darwinism and other related notions
have, however, performed a useful function in juristic thought.
They have taught us the interdependence and the interaction
of all human behavior, and the mistake of seeking to sum up
such widespread activity within the confines of our traditional
juristic formulae. Law is a part of society, and if we see only
the legal proposition or a relationship of sovereign and subject
we see a great deal less than the whole of the law, and we are
more than likely not to see any change at all.

4 *Reason and Nature* (1931) 285.
5 Hegel, *The Philosophy of History* (1900) 55.
6 Morgan, *Evolution and Genetics* (1925) 13.

We are thus driven back to viewing behavior as an activity which has occurred or is occurring. It may represent a process, an evolutionary movement, even progress, but we are without knowledge to make such an assertion. We must look at activity *per se*, realizing at the same time that it is not exclusively a state or condition but a web of interaction in which changes may be taking place which have significance for all our efforts at understanding. It will also be necessary to devise a workable classification of the types of activity we choose to consider, activity which is consistent with the legal system in which it occurs, activity which is inconsistent, activity which accommodates and activity which deters. Social theory is full of attempted classifications but none of them appears readily adaptable to legal inquiry.

THE SYSTEM OF LEGAL RELATIONS

If we were to embark upon the study of a newly-found community of social insects, our first efforts would be directed towards discovering the behavior habits of its members. Later we would attempt to systematize our observations, to see the behavior of the individual members of the community in its relation to that of other members and to that of the community as a whole. In the study of human behavior, however, in its relationship to legal systems we can reverse that process. Already we possess a sufficient knowledge of certain legal systems to permit us to begin with the relationship rather than the activity. This permits us to utilize without waste the results of the vast amount of historical research which now exists.

There are many kinds of relationships, but only a few are essential for the purposes of this inquiry.[7] Of any system of law we want to know over what geographical area it functions. This involves a relationship of space. Some systems may be wholly contained within a particular area or may operate

[7] For a description of most of those which are important for social theory, see Eubank, *Concepts of Sociology* (1932) 308 *et seq.*

upon its members with respect to certain aspects of it, wherever they may be in the world. We want to fix the time of the system, which introduces the temporal relationship. Reciprocity is a third relationship and is present in all social life. It is a movement of interaction resulting in modification. These relationships are physical; in society, however, the psychic plays an equally important part. Societary relationships are primarily mental and involve a relationship of mental interaction. Four notions are customarily employed to account for societary relationship:[8] the idea of contact, or communication among minds; the idea of isolation, or the state of absence of intercommunication or a partial failure of communication; the idea of association or a state of interaction and collective action; and finally the idea of social distance, or the description of the degree of the relationship, which may be intimate, formal, customary or otherwise.

These are the root ideas at the basis of the notion of relationship. Above all, however, we must begin with a complete description of the system of legal relationships. We want to know who acts in the system, when he acts, how he acts, what tools he employs and if he acts with any objective in view. If we know those things we possess a fairly substantial basis upon which to inaugurate our inquiry. We then ask: What is the activity which occurs in this system? Our concern is only with what actually takes place under that particular system. At this point we are not concerned with relations of cause and effect, what makes the system operate or for what purpose, and why it is changing. These are questions which belong if at all to the distant future of knowledge. Our task is great enough if we confine our energies to the inquiry proposed.

We must, however, make provision for the phenomena of change, and, since we cannot introduce any sensible meaning into the notion of cause and effect, we must devise a method which accounts for change without employing that notion. If

[8] *Ibid.* 315.

we encounter change we ask: What is the change in the system? What is the change if any in the activity? Changes in the various systems of the common law, together with concomitant changes in behavior, occurred at the time of the Lancastrian experiment, the accession of the Tudors, in the period of the Stuarts, during the industrial revolution and at other times. The observable changes in behavior which accompanied those changes in the system may be due to that fact or the changes in the system may be due to the changes in behavior, or both or either may be due to other circumstances. That problem, if it is a real one, i.e., capable of solution, is outside the domain of legal inquiry. Our problem as jurists is to provide for the fact of change in the domain of law. We accomplish that task when we state how it occurs. Why it occurs, assuming that in some ultimate sense change does actually occur, is at present unanswerable and seems likely to remain so.

IDEAL TYPES

It is important to note that the study of behavior in its totality in carefully circumscribed systems of legal relations may yield valuable comparisons. Classical anthropology relied heavily upon a comparative method, the essence of which consisted of the collection of numerous detached examples from many cultures, both related and unrelated, to substantiate generally a particular point of view. No effort was made to appraise their validity, to determine if they stood for the point for which they were cited in terms of their actual operation in the culture from which they were drawn, or to estimate the trustworthiness of the report in which they were found. Although the method is still employed its use has been greatly reduced generally since its rejection by Durkheim,[9] and is applied today chiefly to consideration of special points and not to the construction of systems of cultural evolution. Its chief weakness is the doubtfulness of the material it brings together and the danger that the instances will be employed

[9] *Les formes élémentaires de la vie religieuse* (1912).

to bolster preconceived or "library" theories of development. Nevertheless, a sound comparative method ought to take us beyond mere historicism and for that reason the possibility of devising one should never be overlooked. If the method suggested above is followed, it is not unlikely that it may provide a basis for the construction of a comparative system. It is possible that the proper classification of the results of the study of behavior in the systems of legal relations may reveal the presence of units which can be utilized as fixed points to measure motion or change in the total configuration of the systems. It is even conceivable that two extreme points may be found, either actually or as limits, between which the known systems may be arranged in an orderly series. As was observed earlier, however, we must always be prepared for the circumstance that the order of each system is unique and will reveal no basis for comparison. Recourse to this method of comparison has already been made in a few instances. Henry Adams [10] thought that the century 1150–1250 represented the point of history when man held the highest idea of himself as a unit in a unified universe, and that he might use this century as the point from which to measure motion down to Twentieth Century multiplicity, "without assuming anything as true or untrue, except motion." He thought that with the help of these two points of relation he might project his lines forward and backward indefinitely. In his hands, however, the method hardly passed beyond the limits of a literary device. A large-scale application of the method has been attempted by Toynbee [11] in his massive study of civilization. He isolates twenty-one societies in world history [12] which he believes represent

[10] The Education of Henry Adams (1918) 434.
[11] A Study of History (2nd ed. 1935).
[12] The twenty-one societies are: Egyptiac; Andean; Sinic; Minoan; Sumeric; Mayan; Syriac; Indic; Hittite; Hellenic; Western; Orthodox Christian (in Russia); Far Eastern (in Korea and Japan); Orthodox Christian (main body); Far Eastern (main body); Iranic; Arabic; Hindu; Yucatec; Babylonic. 1 Ibid. 133.

"intelligible fields of historical study" and which he utilizes as the basis of comparative study. Since six only of the projected nine volume work have appeared, it would be premature to estimate the success of the undertaking. The proposed method has been most carefully analyzed by Becker,[13] whose studies, however, have not yet been completed, although he has concluded that it represents a genuinely comparative method.

It must be emphasized that abstractions derived from the study of isolated systems of legal relations will always remain ideal entities or limits. There is, however, nothing fallacious in such a result; science would be seriously hampered if it were forced to dispense with idealizations. Its customary procedure is to discover new facts about particular things by analyzing entities which have an altogether different kind of existence. It is a serious error, however, to follow James and Bergson in their view of abstractions as a "spectral dance of bloodless categories." Ideal entities are simply the aspects of a situation which may be treated separately, but which do not actually represent any concrete entity. Thus, perfect solids, perfect gases, rigid bodies are all ideal entities but their utilization has been essential in scientific thought. They represent an effort to distinguish what is relevant from what is irrelevant. With their aid we are able to devise typical situations which permit us to explore conditions of great complexity. In law, in one aspect, they would depict the repetitive elements found in all behavior. Traditional jurisprudence is full of ideal-typical constructions, attempts to reduce the whole of law to a few elements—rights, ownership, liability, persons and so on. They have been, and will always continue to be, notions of great value in the effort to see the apparent complexity of legal phenomena in simple but comprehensive terms capable of multitudinous transformations. Ideal types

[13] 1 Barnes and Becker, *Social Thought from Lore to Science* (1938) 760 *et seq.* Gottschalk, *The Potentialities of Comparative History,* Bulletin of the Society for Social Research, March, 1936.

are heuristic constructions, not, as Becker observes, statistical
modes or averages; they are drawn from empirical reality and,
while they may not represent any part of it in its concrete
form, they enlarge our understanding and control of it, and in
some cases assign actual limits, as in the instance of a perfect
vacuum.

The order found to prevail in the culture area in which a
system of legal relations is isolated will, together with its opposite "disorder," be ideal typical constructions. That order,
as we have seen, is an achievement of the society in which it
is found. It means that human behavior in the society may be
expected to conform to its requirements and that, when it
does not, the agencies of the law may be called into operation.
Law functions either to preserve the orderliness of the system
through knowledge or habit and without the intervention of a
law officer, as when a deed or contract is prepared by the
parties in the required form, or to compel conformity through
the instrumentality of a law agency, as in most court proceed-
ings. In both cases disorder is what is sought to be avoided.
Whether it will be possible ultimately to express in a unitary
principle the multitudinous orders which prevail in each system remains to be determined. An advantage of the ideal
typical method is that the entities if properly constructed are
simple and their meaning fully stated by their definition. At
the same time the phenomena from which they are abstracted
are infinitely complex, and we cannot expect to embrace all
that confronts us in any single formula. Nor should we desire
to do so, since we would never escape from the morass of historicism. Ideal entities embodying the orders of legal relations take us to the relevant in the enormous varieties of social
life and permit us to make comparisons which may possibly
lead to generalization and ultimately to knowledge, universality and system.

9.

THE RELATIONS OF ORDERS

LAW IS BUT ONE of the many systems of order which operate in society. Order of some kind appears to be, as we have seen, an indispensable prerequisite to social existence, but not necessarily the order we know as legal. This is recognized even in the philosophical theory of anarchy, which substitutes universal consent for force as the basis of order, and by Rousseau and his followers, who locate the basis of the necessary order in the "general will." Hence a full understanding of law demands that account be taken of the other systems of order prevailing in society. We need to know the extent of the interaction, if any, between them and the legal order, and the consequences of such interaction. No more important problem confronts the legal theorist. At the same time, none is more difficult. Since the Greeks it has been an endless source of bafflement. Multitudes of solutions have been proposed but none has found general acceptance. It is impossible here to do more than to indicate some of the difficulties which stand in the way of a satisfactory solution.

The difficulty has its origin partly in a conviction and partly in observation, namely, the idea that social phenomena as they represent themselves in particular societies are more or less a unity. There is supposed to be and, indeed, in many cases there apparently is, an observed correlation between phenomena. Weber's [1] study of the extent to which Protestantism took part in the qualitative formation and the quantitative expansion of capitalism throughout the world is an example of an apparently successful correlation. In its most general form, as developed by philosophers and scientists, it is asserted that the supposed unity of social phenomena extends to the entire universe and that everything in it is part of an integrated whole, and is indissolubly joined together, with a consequent action and reaction of one part upon another. This may be so; but it seems wiser to keep the discussion on as concrete a level as possible and confine it to what we think we can observe.

Correlations between phenomena have been attempted in all spheres of the external world. We may divide the world roughly into the physical, the biological, the psychical and the social. In the physical sphere we have attempts—to confine ourselves to legal phenomena alone—to establish correlations between geographical factors and law; in the biological realm, we have efforts to establish the dependence of law upon factors of race, and biological principles such as evolution; from the psychical point of view great pains have been taken to find a correlation between law and the products of "desires," "interests," "wishes" and similar psychical agencies; and in the social world much energy has been expended in the establishment of relationships between law and economics, law and religion, and the other orders which obtain in society. The merits of many of these studies are large; at the least they show us that law is not an isolated phenomenon and that, if it is to accomplish its ends, it must take account of many conflicting desires. None of the attempts at correlation, however, has solved the basic problem of social interdependence. So far as that is concerned, we are, like Dante, lost in the midst of a dark wood; more desperate than he, we have no Virgil in view to guide us to the light.

[1] *The Protestant Ethic and the Spirit of Capitalism* (1930).

It is necessary to state the problem specifically before we examine the more important attempts at its solution. Undeniably many factors influence the characteristics exhibited by any legal system. The political views of judges, their economic predilections, their conceptions of right and wrong together with many other factors all influence the course of judicial decision. A similar process operates in the legislative field. Instances of the process are too well-known to need citation. But, unless we can generalize the process, we are confronted merely with historicism. At best, even that reed is of the slimmest variety. To what extent were the common law judges influenced by economic motives in the establishment of the fellow-servant rule? Our answer will depend upon our premises; and, so far, they have always remained within the domain of the speculative. The difficulties in the way of the establishment of so-called "historical facts" have been well exposed by Carl Becker.[2] He selected one of the simplest and most generally accepted "facts" he could recall in history, namely, the statement that Caesar crossed the Rubicon. He showed the almost insuperable difficulties of determining how, when or why Caesar crossed the Rubicon; and the estimation of the importance of the event varied with the subjective proclivities of the commentator. He showed, moreover, that the event was essentially irrelevant, except as one element in a larger historical pattern which it would be difficult, if not impossible, to recapture completely. "A thousand and one lesser 'facts' went to make up the one simple fact that Caesar crossed the Rubicon," Becker wrote, "and if we had someone, say James Joyce, to know and relate all these facts, it would no doubt require a book of 794 pages (*i.e. Ulysses*) to present this one fact that Caesar crossed the Rubicon." We may pass

[2] Professor Becker's paper "What Are Historical Facts?" read before the American Historical Association in 1926 has not been printed. It is, however, carefully summarized in Barnes, *A History of Historical Writing* (1937) 267-68 upon which the above account is based.

over this difficulty, however, and consider the need for generalization.

Assuming it can be established that in the construction of a particular rule of law judges were influenced by their economic predilections, does this prove anything of importance? First, it may be a disproof of an attempted generalization of the kind "Judges decide cases exclusively upon the basis of prior decisions." Second, it may be the basis of a generalization itself: "Judges do not decide cases exclusively upon the basis of prior decisions." Unless we can generalize our knowledge, however, the occurrence of a single event is of little significance. We generalize in order to predict and sometimes we can do that in the presence of an isolated event, as in a so-called crucial experiment. But the mere "fact" *qua* "fact" usually tells us little. Poincaré [3] brings this out in an amusing anecdote. Carlyle somewhere remarked: "Nothing but facts are of importance. John Lackland passed by here. Here is something that is admirable. Here is a reality for which I would give all the theories in the world." But Carlyle, Poincaré points out, was a fellow countryman of Bacon, and Bacon would not have said that. That is the language of the historian. The scientist would have said: "John Lackland passed by here; that makes no difference to me, for he will never pass this way again." Without generalization we possess only the rudiments of science. Stated another way, our concern with events is whether knowledge of them reveals knowledge of any kind of the likelihood of others. The theory of causality is only important, Keynes [4] points out, because it is thought that by means of its assumptions light can be thrown by the experience of one phenomenon upon the expectation of another.

Three attempts to solve the problem are dominant in social thought: monistic causality, functional dependence and the theory of equilibrium.

[3] *The Foundations of Science* (1921) 128.
[4] *A Treatise on Probability* (1921) 277.

MONISTIC CAUSALITY

In an earlier chapter the difficulties which stand in the way of a sound theory of causation have been indicated. Not least among them is the circumstance that the term "causality" has no generally agreed meaning. Long ago W. K. Clifford pointed out that Aristotle employed it in forty-eight senses and Plato in sixty-four. No one knows how many have been added since they lived. We need not, however, enter into the controversy with respect to its proper meaning. It will be sufficient if we describe how the notion in some of its aspects is employed in legal and social thought.

Elsewhere, the notion of causation is used in many senses in social theory. We need look, however, only at the attempts to give the theory of causation a general form. To say that the total environment—physical, biological, psychical and social—is the cause of a particular event is obviously unsatisfactory; from such a proposition we could deduce nothing with respect to the probability of the occurrence of any event. The theory, therefore, when the need for generalization is felt, takes a monistic form. It is asserted that single elements, or sometimes several elements, are the cause of all legal and social phenomena. The classical attempt to formulate a theory of geographical determinism is Hippocrates' treatise entitled *Influences of Atmosphere, Water and Place* which dates from the Fifth Century B.C. and in which he endeavors to establish a correlation between character elements and the physical environment. Since the time of Hippocrates the notion of geographical determinism has been an almost irresistibly fascinating one to social thinkers; but the results it has yielded have been in inverse proportion to the amount of attention it has received. Demolins' studies indicate the extreme to which modern thought has carried the subject. He asserts categorically that the primary and decisive cause of the civilization of a people is the route which they have followed in their migrations.[5] His arguments exhibit great plausibility, but upon reflection, as Pareto remarks, we begin to put question marks where we have been putting periods. Undoubtedly, specific studies of the influence of various aspects of the environment upon separate elements of behavior—such as the influence of climate and the seasons upon crime and suicide—have added materially to knowledge although the conclusions they attempt to establish are far from proved.

Attempts have been made to establish correlations between legal phenomena and environmental influences. Montesquieu [6] and Buckle [7] thought that in some respects there was a direct connection, although their chief emphasis was on the factor of climate. Randall,[8] in what appears to be the only existing systematic study of the subject, offers a number of interesting suggestions for further investigation, and he concludes that it can be fairly claimed on behalf of the geographic method that it is likely to throw considerable light upon the phases of culture that are embodied in legal rules. Certain obvious and direct relationships between law and geography have long been noted. It is clear that the maritime law of Bolivia and Switzerland will be rudimentary; that the law of a pastoral community will differ from that of an agricultural; that of one based on tree cultivation from one based on corn raising; and that of industrial and trading communities from all others. Blackstone [9] pointed out that "in the Isle of Man, to take away a horse or ox was no felony, but a trespass, because of the difficulty in that little territory to conceal them or to carry them off; but to steal a pig or a fowl, which is easily done,

[5] 1 *Comment la Route Crée le Type Social* (n.d.) vii.

[6] *The Spirit of Laws* (Bohn. ed. 1909) Bk. I, c. iii.

[7] 1 *History of Civilization* (World's classics ed. 1925) c. ii.

[8] *Law and Geography* (1918) 3 Evolution of Law 198. *See also* 3 Wigmore, *A Panorama of the World's Legal Systems* (1928) 1133; idem, *A Map of the World's Law*, 19 Geographical Review (1929) 114; Dubbs, *The Unfolding of Law in the Mountain Region* (1926) 3 Colorado Magazine 113.

[9] Quoted Semple, *Influences of Geographic Environment* (1927) 40.

was a capital misdemeanor, and the offender punished with death." The influence of the sea in this island of fishermen is apparent in the customary form of oath. The judges or deemsters swear to execute the laws as impartially "as the herring's backbone doth lie in the middle of the fish." Manifestly, a multitude of such relationships exist between law and geography. An instance of a systematic attempt in this direction is Pound's [10] hypothesis of the pioneer influence on American jurisprudence. Pound has shown that the two great generic forms of human habitation, urban and rural life, have had a direct effect upon the development of American law. Our American common-law polity reflects the spirit of the pioneer; "it presupposes," he writes, "an American farming community of the first half of the nineteenth century; a situation as far apart as the poles from what our legal system has had to meet in the endeavor to administer justice to great urban communities at the end of the nineteenth and in the twentieth century."

However important specific studies of correlation between social phenomena and the environment [11] may be, we may

[10] *The Spirit of the Common Law* (1921) c. v.

[11] It is interesting to note that in geography as well as in law there has been a separation of "pure" and "applied" science. "For centuries two conceptions of geography have been opposed to each other," Brunhes writes (*Human Geography* (1920) 29), "by generalizing and perhaps stretching the facts a bit, one might be called the Greek conception, the other the Roman conception. The Greek conception was loftier and truer. The Greek geographers, Thales of Miletus, Eratosthenes, Hippocrates, and Aristotle, were philosophers. They had a general, philosophic conception of the physical universe and they sought *before everything else* to work out the natural succession of phenomena and how these phenomena were subordinated to each other. Then came the Romans with their utilitarian spirit; their geography was *practical*. They established itineraries, and composed topographical dictionaries; they were especially dominated by commercial interests, by administrative problems, or by ambitions of conquest. From that time general and speculative geography was neglected; the spirit of geographical science and the taste for it were lost. Only a few men, as rare as they were farseeing, strove to preserve the scientific point of view in geography." (Author's italics.)

dismiss the claim to regard the geographic factor as the unitary cause upon two grounds, among many: (1) The claim has not been proved. Careful geographers such as Brunhes readily admit this, and the arguments of those who deny it are too speculative for serious consideration. (2) Even if we admit a geographical influence it is plainly not monistic in character. Otherwise similar geographic conditions should produce similar cultures; but that this is not the case is clear from many examples, of which the diversity between the Indian cultures of North America and the present-day cultures which have developed under the identical geographical environment may be cited as sufficient. Similar considerations apply to efforts to find a single determiner in the biologic and psychic fields. The study of race in its physical aspects is rapidly approaching, if indeed it has not already achieved, the status of a valid descriptive science. No attempt is made from this direction, however, to establish correlations. It is the innate characters of races which are supposed to be the determiners. That aspect of the matter, however, is still so rudimentary and contradictory, so charged with subjective inferences, that all correlations proposed are wholly suspect. Biologic phenomena also take another form. It is assumed that, since man is an organism, society, which is composed of organisms, should itself be subject to biological laws. The fallacious logic of such an argument, to say nothing of the failure of this analogy in specific cases, is apparent. On the psychical side there are efforts to explain all social phenomena in terms of instincts or their opposite, the conditioned reflex. Both theories, in their general form, whatever may be their particular merits, may be disposed of upon the ground that they fail to account for the infinitely numerous forms of behavior which are expressions of instincts supposed to be constant or of conditioned reflexes which operate under similar conditions. That is to say, in the case of an instinct we have a constant cause producing opposite effects, and in the case of a conditioned reflex we have entirely different behavior by persons subjected to similar conditions. Theories of determinism based on biologic and psychic factors have been introduced into legal thought but, as they are subject to the infirmities outlined, it would serve no useful purpose to summarize them. This is not to say that biological and psychological principles should not be noticed in analyses of legal and social phenomena. They are a necessary and valid factor in social interpretation, and their employment under conditions of proper handling is beyond dispute.

What has been said with respect to monistic causality in the physical, biological and psychical fields is applicable equally to monistic interpretations drawn from social phenomena itself. Claims for many factors as single determiners have been advanced. Law itself, or more properly the notion of the just law, has been held to be such a factor by Stammler.[12] The idea, he wrote, has been "shown to be the fundamental element for the problem of understanding the whole of social history as a unity." We need, however, glance only at the doctrine of historical materialism, the theory which has received the greatest amount of critical attention at the hands of social and legal thinkers. This theory asserts that the general character of a society is determined by the mode of economic production. In its present-day form the theory admits that other factors exercise a conditioning influence but it maintains that the mode of production is the sole factor in the determination of the general character of a society. This theory has received explicit recognition in jurisprudence. Thus, Laski[13] writes: "The law of any given age is a function of the way in which economic power is distributed in that age. The substance of law, broadly speaking, will be determined by the wants and needs of those who dominate the economic system at any given time . . . what the courts do day by day is to apply rules the object of which is to protect the interests of the existing order. . . . In a bourgeois State you will get

[12] *The Theory of Justice* (1925) 485.
[13] *Studies in Law and Politics* (1932) 278.

bourgeois justice; in a communist State you will get communist justice." A similar view was put forward by Brooks Adams [14] many years ago in his assertion that the rules of law are established by the self-interest of the dominant class. A serious difficulty with this view is the ambiguity of the terms employed. What precisely is "bourgeois justice," "communist justice," and "self-interest of the dominant class"? Unless we know the significance of these terms, the assertions are too vague to be of any use. Since the assertions purport to speak of day-to-day decisions, it is legitimate to inquire upon what basis it is possible to predict the outcome of any case, or even the development of a system of law in a particular field. Since the United States is a bourgeois society and the U.S.S.R. the nearest approach to a communist one, the outcome of similar cases in the two societies ought to be different. Both societies, however, have adopted similar rules with respect to abortion, euthanasia and similar controversial subjects. Moreover, the theory fails to explain how the same cause can produce diverse effects. Courts of neighboring states frequently reach opposite conclusions on similar facts when no discernible division of interests is involved. Many scholars have attacked the examples of class interest in the law adduced by the historical materialists by showing that other circumstances more properly account for the event. This argument, however, merely returns us to Becker's position with respect to the "myth" of historical facts. That other circumstances exist shows only that the historical materialists *may* be wrong; it does not show that they *are* wrong, or that their opponents' interpretation is the correct one or that there is not some other view which is still sounder.

Many other valid objections may be urged against historical materialism, including an inquiry into the validity of its necessary premises, *e.g.*, that culture is a unified whole, that the mode of production expresses the entire realm of economics, etc. It should not be overlooked, however, that whatever the

[14] *Centralization and the Law* (1906) 45, 63.

defects of the general theory, it has succeeded, like other interpretations, in directing the attention of the legal scientist to elements in the social structure which are ignored at the risk of incompleteness. Moreover, since it represents the most clearly formulated of all monistic interpretations, it raises more precisely than any of its rivals the essential defect of all such theories. They allow no room for interaction and reciprocity. They adopt a view of causation which is strictly one way and irreversible. But societary phenomena as we observe them do not follow this course. There is constant interaction and reciprocity. Man is aways at work changing the physical environment in which he finds himself and thus modifying whatever influence it may exert upon him. A similar activity takes place in the economic world. If we assume that the relations of production were responsible for the development of the idea of a corporation in modern law, it cannot be denied that that idea has profoundly influenced the relations of production.

FUNCTIONAL DEPENDENCE

To escape from the difficulties engendered by the monistic, irreversible view of causality, the notion of functional dependence has been developed. It is similar to Mill's method of concomitant variations, which asserts that whatever phenomenon varies in any manner, whenever another phenomenon varies in some particular manner, is either a cause or an effect of that phenomenon, or is connected with it through some fact of causation. But the idea of cause and effect, outside of common-sense experience, is, as we have seen, of little help, and Mach and others have urged its complete elimination. Increasing reliance is placed upon the substitute idea of functional dependence which expresses a relationship between events of the kind that when one varies in a determinate manner the other also varies in a determinate manner. Thus disposition may be considered as a function of digestion and digestion may be considered as a function of disposition. No notion of cause and effect is necessarily present. If we apply the idea to economic and legal relations we can represent it symbolically by $l = f(e)$ or vice versa $e = f'(l)$. What we are asserting here is that law varies with economic changes, and economic changes vary with legal changes. Many combinations of variables are possible and we could construct symbolically an extensive system employing all the causal factors suggested in the history of social thought.[15]

It is apparent, however, that the idea for all its improvements upon the notion of monistic causality has serious defects and must be sharply limited in its application. This is made clear by the misleading character of the mathematical symbolization, which is a reversible process. Thus $l = f(e)$ is equivalent to $e = f'(l)$. While that is true in many cases, it is not true in all. Changes in the legal system may take place upon the occurrence of changes in the economic system; but it does not follow that the reverse is true. There may be a one-sided dependence or the dependence may be on both sides. We need to keep before us in a general theory of society the possibility that both events may be present.

In addition, since neither l nor e represents quantities capable of numerical expression, except in relatively unimportant cases, the formula is outside the realm of mathematics at least in its applied sense. It suggests therefore only a method of reasoning and not a mathematical operation. However, the method itself is important; it is a contribution towards the elimination of the defects of the method of monistic causality. It results in the elimination of the doctrine of cause and effect from legal thinking and the fallacies that doctrine has engendered generally. It leaves us in the position taken in the preceding chapter with the addition, however, of an extension in two directions. Not only do we ask: What is the change in the legal system? What is the change if any in the activity? we ask further: What is the change in the economic (or re-

[15] See generally, Hook, *art. Determinism* 5 *Ency. Social Sciences* (1931) 110.

ligious, political, etc.) system? What is the change in the legal system, and the change if any in the activity? Furthermore, we may reverse the questions, which may not only have the effect of revealing important implications of the legal system but may also raise directly the technological question of the effectiveness of law in action.

Even with these limitations the idea represents a distinct advance over the earlier notion of cause and effect. It does not, however, meet the problem of the determination of the factors which are to be regarded as important for the purposes of correlation. The only method which suggests itself here is that of hypothesis and verification. It has been assumed throughout that law is a function of disorder. Order is the element in which it is assumed change must occur for a change to take place in a legal system. Furthermore, the disorder may take place in any of the orders established in society, whether physical, biological, psychical or social. This does not mean that all disorder results in variations in the legal system; only that some disorder, of a kind yet to be determined, can be established in a relationship of correlation.

THE THEORY OF EQUILIBRIUM

Equilibrium is another notion which has been employed to account for the relations of social orders and, like its predecessors, has been taken over from the physical sciences. In that field it refers, in simple terms, to a condition of balance. The equilibrium of a body is stable, if upon slight displacement, forces operate to decrease the displacing impetus; it is unstable if they increase the displacing impetus; it is neutral if they do neither. A weight suspended at rest from a string is an example of the first; a cone balanced on its point the second; and a ball lying on a level table the third. Galileo discovered that the necessary mathematical condition is that the resultant force in any direction is zero. In the Nineteenth Century, particularly in the latter half, the theory of equilibrium was elaborately developed by Clausius and Willard Gibbs,

among others. Modern physical chemistry owes much of its
success to the equations developed by Gibbs in this field.
Mechanical analogies were eagerly utilized by the two
leaders of Nineteenth Century social thought—Comte and
Spencer. This can perhaps be explained by the fact that the
early instruction or experiences of both directly influenced
their choice of analogies. Comte was trained at the École
Polytechnique and supported himself early in life by giving
lessons in mathematics. It is not surprising, therefore, to discover him employing the notions of statics and dynamics in
his system—statics to the theory of the social order and dynamics to the theory of progress. Spencer was largely self-
taught, but for the nine years preceding his entrance upon his
life work he was employed in an engineering capacity by one
of the English railroads. He thought of statics as the study of
the equilibrium of a perfect society and of dynamics as the
methods or means utilized to reach that state. The idea of
equilibrium was also taken up by the mathematical economists
—Walras and Pareto among others—and is now employed ex-
tensively in social thought, including jurisprudence.

It represents in social theory a method of studying the in-
terrelations of social phenomena and particularly, in the hands
of certain thinkers, an effort to escape the dangers inherent in
viewing interdependence as a relation of cause and effect
only. Unfortunately, the idea of equilibrium has no generally
accepted meaning in social thought. The question of the
necessity of the notion in social theory recently has been thor-
oughly debated in the pages of the *Revue Internationale de
Sociologie*.[16] Duprat, who initiated the discussion, rejected
the utilization of the mechanical and physio-chemical theories
of equilibrium in social thought but pleaded for its employment in one of its numerous social senses. Sorokin thought its

[16] Duprat, *Introduction à l'étude des "équilibres sociaux"*; Sorokin,
Le concept d'équilibre est-il nécessaire aux sciences sociale?; Lasbax,
La sociologie et la notion d'équilibre (1936) 44 Revue Internationale de
Sociologie, Nos. IX-X.

use in any of its social senses was an illusion and that it ought to be eliminated from the social sciences. Lasbax endeavored, not at all persuasively, to salvage from the wreckage of Sorokin's barrage some useful aspect of the theory. With his customary industry Sorokin classified the five meanings in which the notion of equilibrium is employed: (1) Conceptions identifying equilibrium with a state of rest. It was in this sense that it was employed by Spencer, Marshall, J. S. Clark, Pareto and others. Thus, Spencer wrote, "In all cases, then, there is a progress towards equilibration. That universal co-existence of antagonistic forces which, as we saw before, necessitates the universality of rhythm, and which, as we saw before, necessitates the decomposition of every force into divergent forces, at the same time necessitates the ultimate establishment of a balance. Every motion being motion under resistance is continually suffering deductions; and these unceasing deductions finally result in the cessation of motion." It is also in this sense that it has recently been introduced into jurisprudence.[17] (2) Conceptions identifying equilibrium with a state of rest in the sense of some moral or other valuation. Thus Marshall [18] writes: "A business firm grows and attains strength, and afterwards perhaps stagnates and decays; and at the turning point there is a balancing or equilibrium of the forces of life and decay." Jevons, Fetter, Pigou, Pareto and others have used it in this sense. (3) Conceptions identifying equilibrium and the mutual or inhibiting limitation of two or more social organs, functions, activities or forces. This is perhaps best exemplified by the so-called doctrine of the balance of powers. (4) Conceptions of equilibrium identifying it with "adaptation," "adjustment," "maximum utility," "normality," "harmony," "utility," "aptitude," "efficacy," "survival," "suum cuique," and other normative and other evaluative notions (Comte, Spencer, Marshall and others). (5) Conceptions of equilibrium identifying it with a tendency of

[17] Timasheff, The Sociology of Law (1939) 21 and c. xi.
[18] Principles of Economics (8th ed. 1930) 323.

the whole social system when it is disturbed to return to an anterior state or to maintain its orientation or its "normal" level. Pigou, Marshall and Pareto use it in this sense. This is also one of its meanings in jurisprudence.[19] It is to be noted that the same writer uses the notion in several senses. This, however, is not a ground for criticism so long as the writer's meaning is clear.

The weaknesses of the theory of equilibrium are readily apparent.[20] In its scientific use one of its main functions is measurement, which means, among other things, the establishment of a relationship between numbers and objects or events. In mathematical economics an attempt is now being made to develop a technique for the substitution of statistical quantities for the abstractions in which the theory of equilibrium is formulated. In the absence of a sound development in this direction we are left at best with a logical (not a mathematical) method to be applied to the most dubious concepts and tendencies. It is popularly supposed that Edgeworth in his *Mathematical Psychics* (1881) validated the legitimacy of such a method but his own efforts to apply it to the Hedonistic calculus should be a sufficient warning of the dangers which may overcome the unwary. Even Pareto,[21] who in his time was among those who carried the method furthest in economics, rejected it in its full application in social theory because of its lack of susceptibility to mathematical treatment. To assert as Spencer does that a perfect society is in "balance" is to speak in figurative terms which are unnecessary and only confusing. In a limited sense it might be possible to work out a "balance" between population and production, since these elements can be counted; but how, except in some subjective sense, could a "balance" ever be determined between religious and ethical phenomena or between legal and

[19] *Op. cit. supra* note 17.

[20] For detailed criticisms of the notion in its five senses, see Sorokin, *op. cit. supra* note 16.

[21] 3 *The Mind and Society* (1935) 1192.

economic phenomena? What does Timasheff's assertion that "the property of every concrete system is to return to an original situation, if comparatively small disturbances have taken place" mean when applied to social phenomena? He states that we have "small disturbances" if the forces creating the interdependence of the elements of the system are stronger than the forces causing the disturbance. These statements are too lacking in precision, however, to be employed with any general agreement. In what sense does a society ever return to its anterior position? A public official is assassinated and another takes his place. Is it a return, a departure or a continuance? In what sense do elements ever become interdependent? After the Russian Revolution, which would not seem to be a small disturbance, what elements become interdependent? Is there no longer any relationship between legal and ethical phenomena in the U.S.S.R.? Unless the terms we employ are given something other than a figurative meaning the assertions containing them remain as vague and inadequate as the terms themselves. The notion of equilibrium reduces itself merely to another example of the dangers attendant upon the introduction of ideas or words from other sciences. If jurisprudence is to become a true science it must minimize the risk of error by studying the facts which confront it from the position of its own hypotheses.

10.

THE VALUATION OF LEGAL SCIENCE

JURISPRUDENCE AIMS AT THE FORMULATION of true propositions about legal behavior in terms of the elements found in all orders, and the ultimate arrangement of the propositions, or others based upon them, in the form of a logical system. In this respect, jurisprudence follows the example of modern economics, biology, dynamics and other subjects in founding its postulates in the first instance upon observable conditions. In the view of modern mathematics taken by Hilbert, Huntington and others its method is essentially postulational, the postulates being given, and the question of their truth or falsity is held to be completely irrelevant, consistency being in this respect the only admissible test. Modern science, however, whatever may be the case in mathematics, is concerned to a degree at least with the empirical validity of its initial assumptions. If they are once established the method of handling them is inherently dialectical. We are able to visualize more precisely rival possibilities, to observe inconsistencies, to foresee the possible consequences and to perceive new relations in the subject matter of the system. At the same time, the dialectical process must be continuously corrected by observation, and observations continuously refined by dialectical considerations. This necessity is well illustrated by Laplace's [1]

[1] *Traité de mécanique céleste* (2nd ed. 1829) Bk. IV, §§ 15, 23.

analysis of tidal conditions. He first constructed his formulae and then compared them with observations which had been carried on at the harbor of Brest for six consecutive years. These observations revealed that the formulae did not satisfy all the observed phenomena. Further refinements were made in the formulae and the process of checking the formulae with observation was continued by his successors until the corrections became so numerous that an entirely new principle had to be devised. The whole process was completely mutual. Observations suggested corrections in the theory, and corrections in the theory prompted refinements in the observations. Such a procedure seems entirely open to jurisprudence.

Law, however, is a vital element of all social life, and the question arises whether jurisprudence necessarily should be conceived in terms of social function in addition to its purely scientific aims. The study of jurisprudence, as of some other sciences closely connected with social life, may be undertaken for any one or all of several purposes. Jurisprudence may be studied purely as a system of knowledge as an end in itself; it may be extended to a consideration of the application of its established knowledge in its naked scientific aspects to questions of social welfare; and it may be further enlarged to embrace the normative features of collective behavior. These aims are not mutually exclusive, although they may not all be realizable at the same time. The determination of their legitimacy is immediately present in all studies whose subject matter is directly social, although it is not altogether absent in some at least of the other sciences.

KNOWLEDGE

Jurisprudence as the pursuit of truth for its own sake has its justification in the fact that such a procedure gratifies legitimate curiosity. Aristotle [2] long ago observed that "all men by nature desire to know." From Plato to Bertrand Rus-

---

[2] *Metaphysics*, A. 1. 980a.

sell, knowledge has been held to be an ultimate value, important on its own account and not as a means to other things.[3] Similar views are held in Eastern philosophy, although, as in Christianity, the only truth which is permissible is religious truth. In the tradition of Christianity, a knowledge of truth was a necessary element in salvation, but knowledge which was not religious was heretical.[4] In the Platonic view, the desire for knowledge has its impulse in curiosity, the impulse to handle strange and pleasing objects. With most persons the impulse is gratified by handling the object; when the impulse is not thus satisfied the stimulation continues and Plato believed that at this stage the conflict was resolved by rising to the level of generalization.

Modern psychology has not carried the question of the stimulus of curiosity beyond the point where James left it. The Freudians are content to regard the curiosity motive in science as an emanation in large part from childish curiosity with respect to sex. James,[5] however, distinguished sharply between the curiosity exhibited by children and animals in the impulse to touch and feel and scientific curiosity and metaphysical wonder. He pointed out that the stimuli in the latter cases are not objects, but ways of conceiving objects. He believed that the motions and actions they give rise to are to be classed, with many other aesthetic manifestations, sensitive and motor, as incidental features of our mental life. "The philosophic brain," he concluded, "responds to an inconsistency or a gap in its knowledge, just as the musical brain responds to a discord in what it hears." This, of course, is speculative; but present-day knowledge has added little to the discussion.

When we defend as legitimate the justification of jurisprudence as having for its sole aim the pursuit of knowledge it

[3] Plato, *Republic* 475 *et seq.*, 523-b; Russell, *The Problem of China* (1922) 5.

[4] 1 Gibbon, *Decline and Fall of the Roman Empire* (1845) 585.

[5] 2 *Principles of Psychology* (1904) 430.

is not intended to include all knowledge. Much knowledge is without any value whatsoever, and some possesses only utilitarian interest. Knowledge which Plato defended as important on its own account means, however, the knowledge of the external world which is derived from scientific inquiry. That the impulse for knowledge of this sort is closely related to, if indeed it is not a part of, the stimulus which lies behind efforts at artistic contemplation cannot be doubted. We see this fact revealed most clearly, as Russell has observed, in the strangely emotional writings of those Greek philosophers in whom an interest in art and science were united to a degree rarely since witnessed. "The world, which is the same for all," said Heraclitus, "is an ever-living fire, with measures kindling, and measures going out." Under the burden of civilization it is difficult today to reach such levels of intellectual emotion, and we observe it now only in the rare appearance of supreme genius. What we are permitted to glimpse in its purest form in them, however, is represented to a lesser degree in all efforts to understand nature, defective as many of them are. It should not be overlooked also that the pursuit of knowledge for its own sake is strengthened from another direction. Life as it is lived today is a painful spectacle to many men of strongly developed artistic and intellectual impulses. They despair that the world will ever be a place of joy. They are stimulated by the hope that their researches can have no practical application. "This subject," Hardy wrote of pure mathematics, "has no practical use; that is to say, it cannot be used for promoting directly the destruction of human life or for accentuating the present inequalities in the distribution of wealth." Whether derived from this direction or from others, it is certain that the impulse towards a comprehension of nature is a valid one, and as such is its own justification.

SOCIAL WELFARE

Jurisprudence considered as the gratification of intellectual desires is primarily, though not exclusively, an approach founded upon the point of view of the individual scientist. The quest for knowledge, however, is an activity which takes place within the confines of society, which thus has an interest in inquiring whether the activity is harmful or beneficial to it and in what sense. Knowledge the application of which can result only in harm is rare, although such a possibility is not beyond the range of conjecture, e.g., an understanding of techniques whose sole function is the promotion of useless suffering. The damage that knowledge has done to society has generally been the result of its improper application. It is certain that in the field of application we are today face to face with a situation of tremendous gravity and magnitude. In jurisprudence, however, we are still without any real knowledge and the possibility of harmfulness is largely academic. Society's main interest is in the benefits which may be expected from its pursuit.

In the realm of pure science the aim of the scientist is to make discoveries, not to make useful discoveries. It has so happened, however, that the pursuit of science for its own sake has generally yielded results of great practical importance. Existing scientific knowledge consists of much that is without utilitarian significance; but at the same time it contains large areas capable of direct application. Its aspects of practical importance, however, are accidental and unsought, in spite of the fact that they have made possible most of the important transformations in modern living. There is a strong conviction on the part of scientists, which finds considerable support in the history of science, that research directed exclusively to practical ends leads generally to inferior work of only temporary significance.

There is no certainty that the formulation of a pure science of law will duplicate the history of the other so-called pure sciences and yield results of practical importance. At the same time, there is no certainty that it will not. If the construction of a pure science of law should follow the history of other sciences, and the chances seem to be that it will, certain things may reasonably be expected of it. Among those things is an extension of the knowledge it erects to questions of social welfare.

At this point the normative has not yet entered. Whether or not it is ever the concern of the scientist is a question which demands separate consideration. Here the problem is the determination of the nature and legitimacy of the application of legal science to social life.

It is assumed that legal science when it is ultimately formulated will exhibit what appear to be the principal characteristics of all science. That is to say, in essence it will consist of propositions deduced from a series of postulates. It should be emphasized that the postulates are not the so-called "self-evident" axioms whose truth is supposed to be so clear that no rational person would dispute them. Basically, they are hypotheses or assumptions which it is necessary to lay down before any discussion can begin. In no science, not even mathematics, has it yet been possible to state all the assumptions upon which it is grounded and it is perhaps not necessary to do so in order to arrive at truth, although this is still not known. In mathematics the postulate is given; it is accepted without proof. In science and the social sciences, however, the postulate or hypothesis generally involves a relationship to data which gives it a probability of correctness, not, however, in any ultimate sense, but merely in relationship to the data observed. This may be put another way by saying that if the data were different there would be a different hypothesis. Although it is not possible to state all the assumptions in any science, nevertheless the postulates which are agreed upon limit the field of discussion. They constitute the universe of discourse. This is not to say that the deductive process will never yield new discoveries. The history of science contains too many examples to the contrary to give any weight to such a contention. The prediction of the effect of gravitation upon light waves is a familiar and recent example of a discovery reached by the deductive process. No doubt the most difficult task confronting the legal scientist is the selection of the initial postulates. Upon them depends the universe in which he will operate. Like all such postulates they will be of an extreme simplicity and related to data of an apparently readily recognizable kind. Two such postulates which have been assumed throughout this study are: (1) The rules of law which obtain in any society operate to establish a system of order in that society; and (2) One of the methods of meeting disorder in a society is by the establishment of rules of law. In order to have a workable set of postulates many other postulates and definitions must, of course, be stated, e.g., definitions of "order" and "disorder," "rules of law," that there is such an entity as society, etc. Once the postulates are established, however, the legal scientist is in a position to deduce from them a series of propositions of general character. The system of postulates in any science is never fixed, and hence we are continually confronted with new propositions. Some individual of original genius is constantly introducing new definitions and postulates, which give a novel turn to the system.

Many, if not most, of the propositions established by the legal scientist will possess no utilitarian value whatsoever. Some, however, will no doubt be capable of successful application. Temporarily putting to one side questions of the normative, the social function of the propositions of a science of law is to reveal with more or less accuracy the consequences or the antecedents of particular courses of action. That is the substance of the application of the propositions of any science to nature or society. Assuming the establishment of certain propositions, it should be possible upon a close scrutiny of the Constitution of the United States to determine the principal interests and motives of the men who framed it. Again, assuming the establishment of the proposition that the perpetuation of a legal system is dependent on the survival of a highly trained professional class, the consequence of the abolition of such a class in a society means the disappearance of the legal system then obtaining. Whether the legal profession ought to be abolished is a question not before the legal scientist. If the question is whether or not it is to be abolished, the legal scientist can state the effect upon the legal system of its abolition. Such methods are typical of those employed in the "exact sciences." A physicist, accepting Coulomb's two propositions or "laws" with respect to friction, is able to measure it for most practical purposes through the employment of a simple "coefficient of friction." He does not inquire whether it is good or bad to measure the friction.

The extent to which the propositions of a science of law will be applicable to the problems of a particular system is difficult to forecast. It is reasonably certain, however, that they will always remain too general for application to the minutiae of a system, e.g., how a particular judge will decide a particular case. In a famous passage Laplace has well summed up the requirements of a really complete knowledge. "We ought then to regard the present state of the universe as the effect of its anterior state and as the cause of the one which is to follow. Given for one instant an intelligence which could comprehend all the forces by which nature is animated and the respective situation of the beings who compose it— an intelligence sufficiently vast to submit these data to analysis —it would embrace in the same formula the movements of the greatest bodies of the universe and those of the lightest atom; for it, nothing would be uncertain and the future, as the past, would be present to its eyes. The human mind offers, in the perfection which it has been able to give to astronomy, a feeble idea of this intelligence. Its discoveries in mechanics and geometry, added to that of universal gravity, have enabled it to comprehend in the same analytical expressions the past and future states of the system of the world. Applying the same method to some other objects of its knowledge, it has succeeded in referring to general laws observed phenomena and in foreseeing those which given circumstances ought to produce." [6] No such impossible ideal, however, is entertained by science. It would be a desperate and futile task to attempt a perfect description of any phenomenon. No knowledge that we now or are likely to possess will permit us to describe completely the mere act of tossing a pencil to the floor. It is probable that the propositions of a science of law will be highly general at first and concerned only with the simplest situations. Later, other notions will be introduced which will permit a wider range of operations, but in which much will be omitted. Details will continue to be filled in, but the variables which will always remain unaccounted for will make the process a never-ending one.

There appears to be only one ground for questioning the legitimacy of such applications of science. They may bring about results which are offensive to groups in society and conclude in the suppression of large areas of science itself. The safety-lamp minimized the danger of explosion from fire-damp, but since it made possible the more extensive operation of mines it increased the number of men exposed to other hazards. It was not suppressed since a greater production of coal was desired for one or more reasons. There are, however, many well-attested cases of the suppression of inventions,[7] and the difficulties which workers in such a field of research as birth control have had to face are notorious. These dangers are ones which science has always faced and must always be prepared to risk. From its own point of view, however, as distinguished from that of society or groups within society, the legitimacy of the application of its principles hardly seems open to question. It neither hinders nor distorts the scientific program. Such applications as are possible are unsought by-products, and as such stand in the way of nothing the scientist holds necessary to the successful accomplishment of his objectives.

[6] A Philosophical Essay on Probabilities (1902) 4.

[7] Stern, Restraints upon the Utilization of Inventions (1938) 200 The Annals 13, 17.

What has been said so far has been directed solely to the problems of a pure science of law. A technology of law raises its own special problems, and since jurisprudence traditionally, at least in Anglo-American thought, is a technology, it appears unnecessary to consider in detail what has been so abundantly treated elsewhere. Science generally is concerned with an understanding of the external world, using the phrase in a broad sense; technology is directed to immediate improvements in existing processes or thought or to the discovery of new processes or things. There is ample room for both activities, and their relationship is to a considerable degree reciprocal. The end product of both is knowledge, and the triumphs of technology have been of a notable order. A close scrutiny of activities with a view to their direct improvement undoubtedly has suggested problems which might never have occurred to the pure scientist and the solution of which has made possible to a material degree the kind of life we enjoy today. The mathematical analysis of oil films is such a case. In addition, science itself learns from existing technologies. Galileo's study of suction pumps led directly to his and Torricelli's discovery of barometric pressures. Technology is dependent in the main for knowledge first formulated by pure science, but this is not the important point of difference. The significant demarcation between science and technology is that the systematic method of the former results in the inevitable disclosure of breaches in its knowledge, while that of the latter is essentially haphazard and the gap may never be revealed. No amount of research looking toward the improvement of the telephone will ever disclose the principle of radio. Both the principle of the telephone and the radio are within likely reach in the systematic exploration of a field of physics. This principle is receiving explicit recognition today in the researches in pure science maintained by business concerns in industry and agriculture. In modern business the technologist is rapidly disappearing. The inventor of the past finds himself unable to cope with the problems which now confront him, and business has found it profitable if not necessary to establish systematic research in fields which seem remote from all practical application. This is a lesson which the social studies are slow in learning and jurisprudence scarcely at all. There was a beginning in the Institute of Law at the Johns Hopkins University, but it was hardly under way before lack of funds closed its doors and no similar institution has since been started. Two thousand years of research of the kind carried on by traditional jurisprudence, however meritorious it may have been—and its great value is not to be underestimated—should have revealed that it is subject to the definite limits which circumscribe the activities of all technologies.

THE VALUATION OF VALUES

There is a powerful school of thought which insists that science is incomplete to the extent that it ignores values. In opposition it is contended that the aim of science is knowledge, that (for many reasons) questions of value cannot be rationally determined and hence lie outside the realm of knowledge and therefore of science. It is true that the more exact sciences rarely, if ever, pronounce upon ultimate values. When we pass to less rigorous studies—economics, biology, jurisprudence—there is no agreement on the place of the normative in either theory or practice. It is insisted by students in these fields that the subjects cannot be dissociated from ethics, and problems of value are explicitly treated by them in their works; other students vehemently plead for a separation and do their best to eliminate in their own work the valuative element. In the present state of our knowledge it is impossible to bring the matter to a conclusion by any test, either experimental or formal. What follows therefore must be regarded as speculative, although it seems that certain delimitations can be clearly marked out.

At the beginning it should be observed that the customary assertion "propositions involving the verb 'ought,' are different in kind from propositions involving the verb 'is' " is true only if we are dealing with non-determinate systems. Thus Cohen [8] has pointed out that in a completely determinate system "there is no difference of content between the proposition 'If $2ab$ is added to $a^2 + b^2$ the result will be a perfect square' and the proposition 'In order to obtain a perfect square we ought to add $2ab$ to $a^2 + b^2$.'" This does not mean that the teleologic is necessarily completely merged with the mechanistic, but only that no useful purpose would be served by distinguishing between them. In other words, if we view ethics as embracing a general theory of value, "ought" can refer to many standards or ends besides the moral. In the example of the perfect square the ought is logical and envisages consistency or truth, which are both values. If truth is the objective correspondence of thought with fact it has no moral value since it is not dependent upon volition. In a completely determinate system we are at liberty therefore, so far as intent is concerned, to read "it is necessary" wherever we encounter the verb "ought." If we assume a completely determinate system, embracing both the mechanistic and the teleologic, this is true even of such a proposition as "Perfect squares in any quantity always promote the good life and therefore we ought to have as many as possible."

But unless there is included within the determinate system itself either expressly or impliedly a system of values, we cannot introduce the normative element by merely employing the verb "ought." Thus, assuming a determinate system of law in which the normative has been excluded, we are asserting the same thing when we say, "If the highly trained professional class is continued the legal system will be perpetuated" and "In order to perpetuate the legal system we ought to continue the highly trained professional class." All we can mean in such a determinative system by using "ought" is "it is necessary," unless we expressly or impliedly recognize a logical value which may of course be the situation in every case. In

[8] *Law and the Social Order* (1930) 242.

order to get explicitly into the normative we must make some such assertion as "We ought to perpetuate the legal system and therefore let us continue the highly trained professional class." In a determinate system in which value elements have been rigorously excluded, assuming this to be possible, we cannot transform the propositions of the system into normative propositions and stay within the system.

No place has been assigned to the normative in the system of legal science so far envisaged. The question now arises whether it is possible and desirable to construct an adequate science of law completely omitting the normative. As to the possibility, there appears to be no ground for uncertainty. No reason suggests itself why a system of descriptive postulates of the kind "The rules of law which obtain in any society operate to establish a system of order in that society" can not be devised without the introduction of the normative. Such a set of postulates would have as its limit a complete descriptive system. No doubt some postulates will recognize the existence of the normative in all legal systems, but without any attempt at evaluation, e.g., "Legal rules direct what men ought to do." Whether or not a science of law should embrace a valuation of the values which obtain in all legal systems is, however, a more difficult question.

It is advisable to recognize explicitly at the outset the intimate relationship between the law of a society and ethics. Rules of law state as clearly as may be what ought or ought not to happen, even if the "ought" happens to be missing from the pronouncement. With this consideration in mind, the claim of such a careful analyst as Hartmann [9] that "ethics, in fact, must contain the ultimate foundation of law; in its scale of values it must indicate the place for the value of law in general" does not seem extravagant. Nevertheless, in spite of the fact that legal rules are normative, there has been an earnest effort on the part of students of the law to separate

[9] 1 *Ethics* (1932) 109.

them from ethics and view them from an altogether different position. Kant [10] took the view that the distinction was to be found in the different motives of obedience which lie behind the fulfillment of ethical and legal obligations. Austin [11] found the distinction in the circumstance that rules of law flow from a determinate or sovereign source, whereas moral rules do not. Holmes,[12] thinking of the law as "the prophecies of what the courts will do in fact" found only confusion in the introduction of moral notions into such a system and expressed the belief that it would be "a gain if every word of moral significance could be banished from the law altogether, and other words adopted which should convey legal ideas uncolored by anything outside the law." In spite of the extensive discussion which has been generated, the problem still remains.[13] Moreover, we are confronted not only with the realization that legal rules are in themselves norms, but that legal systems are permeated with ethical ideals, expressed and unexpressed. In tort we have the ethical standard of reasonable conduct; in inheritance, that a man ought not to benefit by his own wrong conduct; in contract, that promises ought to be kept except in certain rigidly defined cases. When we are faced with such an intimate relation between law and morals, when it is apparent that what legal students are attempting is to explain why legal norms are not legal norms, it is surprising that the subject is not in a worse state of confusion than exists. The effort to look at legal norms other than from the ethical point of view is no doubt valid and necessary. It must, however, always remain a source of disorder and danger to legal thinking unless a sharper dichotomy is devised. Notwithstanding the great divergence of opinion which exists in the matter, it

[10] *The Philosophy of Law* (1887) 22.

[11] *Lectures on Jurisprudence* (1875) § 143 *et seq.*

[12] *Collected Legal Papers* (1920) 173, 179.

[13] For a recent acute discussion see Yntema, *The Rational Basis of Legal Science* (1931) 31 Col. L. Rev. 925 and the reply of Professor Cohen, *op. cit.* note 8 *ibid.*

should be possible to place the subject on a less perilous basis.

We may begin with three assumptions which seem amply warranted: (1) a postulational science of law is possible; (2) a postulational science of ethics is possible; [14] (3) a postulational science of law and ethics in combination is possible. For present purposes, the entire controversy may be reduced to the question: Is the third possibility necessary and desirable? If we mean: Can we construct a descriptive science of law without the introduction of value elements? then the method of the third procedure is not necessary. In such a case we would limit ourselves to the first possibility. If we mean, however: Can we construct a *complete* descriptive science of law and not introduce value elements? then the third possibility is the one we must adopt. For the fact is that a complete description of any legal system must recognize the presence of two elements in that system: an ethical element and a behavior element. Behavior may be a measure of value, but unless that postulate is assumed which in itself would introduce the normative into the science of law, the legal system is not fully described if the ethical element is omitted. This argument is not met by the fact that "description" is here being used in two senses. It is being employed in its ordinary sense of delineation; in that sense the ethical element could be described in behavioristic terms without the introduction of the normative. By a description of the normative, however, is meant not only its ordinary meaning but, more particularly, the evaluation of values. That is the function of a postulational science of ethics, and it is in that sense that the term "description" is used. In other words, we are without a complete knowledge of legal phenomena in the absence of full behavioristic descriptions and an evaluation of the values of the phenomena. This position, of course, may be maintained only with respect to phenomena which embrace value ele-

[14] For the arguments in support of the second proposition see Cohen, *Reason and Nature* (1931) 427 *et seq.*

ments; it is inapplicable, for example, in the field of mechanics where value elements are completely absent in the phenomena mechanics investigates. But value elements are present in the phenomena which are the subject matter of a science of law, and a description which aims at completeness cannot ignore them. These considerations, however, do not exhaust the inquiry.

We have still to determine whether or not a postulational science of law and ethics in combination is desirable. Of course, since such a union is necessary for completeness, it is also desirable from the point of view of full knowledge. In the controversy over the to-be*ness* or the not to-be*ness* of normative jurisprudence this does not, however, appear to be the point at issue. Rather, it seems to be whether we shall now, as opposed to some future date, evaluate the values of legal phenomena. We must again distinguish here between a science of law and technological jurisprudence. If we look at the question from the first position the task is clearly beyond our powers. We have no knowledge which would permit us to evaluate any of the values of a legal system. The achievement of such knowledge belongs altogether to the future and in its absence the question is completely academic. With technological jurisprudence the case is different. The morality which law reflects is prevalent sentiment; but prevalent sentiment is neither definite nor constant. It is, however, apt to become crystallized in legal systems and thus with the passage of time be out of touch with the new notions of proper behavior. Technological jurisprudence here performs a useful service in criticizing obsolete morality, suggesting methods of adaptation and formulating new standards. A recent notable accomplishment in this field has been its treatment of the freedom of contract doctrine and the subsequent rescue of the courts from a position totally inconsistent with current moral ideas of the community.

Whether, in the construction of a science of law, the postulational scheme should include the normative or whether, for the time being, it should omit it, is a matter of opinion. Legitimate considerations, however, indicate that omission is the wiser course. We have more chance of success if our initial field of inquiry is not too ambitiously staked out. Greek science took in a wide area, but at the end the tangible results were small. Its chief heritage is its point of view. Modern science, however, recognizes the necessity of the specific. It represents, in Santayana's [15] words, "a patient siege laid to the truth, which was approached blindly and without a general, as by an army of ants; it was not stormed imaginatively as by the ancient Ionians, who had reached at once the notion of nature's dynamic unity, but had neglected to take possession in detail of the intervening tracts, whence resources might be drawn in order to maintain the main position." It happened that the discoveries thus made dropped of their own accord into a system, and Descartes and Newton were able to reach a general physics. In the construction of a science of law, however, we have the notion of system uppermost in our minds, and our first efforts are directed to its attainment. At the same time we should not overlook the advantages to be derived from narrowing the field of the specific so far as it is consistent with the idea of system. Legal scientists must face real difficulties in constructing a behavioristic system. They would face even greater difficulties in the formulation of a value system. Such an enterprise would certainly increase the risks of confusion. Moreover, since the behavioristic realm and the value realm are distinct, they can easily be joined at a later time. It is true that such a method has disadvantages. Human life is not compartmentalized, and it well may be that in severing it into units we miss much that is significant. In the Middle Ages, in Western Europe, during the periods when we can discern a unity of thought not paralleled in the modern world, great systems of law, theology and philosophy were constructed which have not been equaled since in breadth or incisiveness. The Renaissance gave us

[15] *Reason in Science* (1935) 6.

freedom to study the specific, but it deprived us of the unity
to see life in its entirety. Whatever doubts may have lingered
with respect to the values of the old method of unity were
dispelled by the Industrial Revolution and the triumphs of
the principle of the Division of Labor. Toynbee has recently
shown the disasters which attend the application of the principle in the field of historical study. Nevertheless, allowing
for all that it lacks in comprehensiveness, its triumphs are
real, and, if used with full awareness of its limitations and
with a constant effort to correct them, its advantages are
plain.

Thus to return to our initial assumptions, jurisprudence as
the pursuit of knowledge justifies itself; its knowledge with
complete propriety may be extended to questions of social
welfare; and ultimately, since it aims at full knowledge, it
must be enlarged to include the normative. In the House of
Jurisprudence, as Pound has said, there are many mansions.
It need only be added that in such diversity it finds its
strength.

INDEX

A

Abstraction, omission of part of truth, 84; ideal types, 110

Activity, and change, 99-106; defined, 100; description of, 101-106; and behavior, 102; as a process, 104; legal relations, 107

Adams, Brooks, materialist conception of history, 4; on economic determinism, 121

Adams, Henry, on comparative method, 109

Administration, as element of legal structure, 96

American legal thought, present-day, 4-7

Analogies, mechanical, 125

Anarchy, philosophical theory of, 112

Anthropology, analysis of social structure, 2

Aquinas, Thomas, on law as order, 25; notion of force, 61

Aristotle, law as order, 24-25;

on decrees of insane despots, 60; notion of force, 61; on activity and relation, 100; forty-eight senses of causality, 116; on knowledge, 130

Associations, as element of legal structure, 95

Assumptions in jurisprudence, 4-7

Austin, John, on law and ethics, 142

B

Barometric pressure, 138

Bateson, W., on transmission of culture, 45; evolution, 105

Becker, Carl, on historical facts, 114, 121

Becker, Howard, on ideal types, 111

Behavior, human, and social sciences, 1-2; orderly, 20-21; defined, 106; and activity, 102; continuous change, 104

Benjamin, A. Cornelius, on discovery, 59

T

Technology, in jurisprudence, 8-9

Testament. *See* Will.

Thurnwald, Richard, on egocentric positions, 22

Tides, analysis of, 130

Timasheff, N. S., theory of equilibrium, 128

Titchener, Edward Bradford, on science and technology, 12

Torricelli, Evangelista, discovery of barometric pressure, 138

Toynbee, Arnold J., examples of historical causation, 66-67; use of comparative method, 109; on division of labor, 146

Tradition, taught, 46

Tutuing, mentioned, 34

Tyler, H. W., notion of force, 62

Types, ideal. *See* Ideal types.

U

Unconscious invention, 58

Universal culture pattern, 18

Utility, in jurisprudence, 132-139

V

Values, valuation of, 139-146

Veblen, Thorstein, on technological adaptation, 67

Verification, nature of, 70-76

Virgil, mentioned, 113

Visconti, Giovanni Maria, insane despot, 60

W

Wallas, Graham, on social heredity, 44, 46; on discovery, 58-59

Walras, Leon, theory of equilibrium, 125

Ward, Lester, notion of force, 61; on desires, 63

Weber, Max, on correlation of social phenomena, 113

Welfare, social, and law, 132-139

Westermarck, Edward, on theory of stages, 26-27; on specialization, 39; on primogeniture, 41; on detailed study of customs, 95

Whitehead, Alfred North, on order of nature, 50; on simple location, 67; on growth of science, 73; on classification, 91; on classes, 93

Wigmore, John H., on survival of legal systems, 47

Will, as invention, 31-37; invention of, 32-37

Wishes, mentioned, 113

Wissler, Clark, on universal culture pattern, 18

World, what made of, 50

Y

Yntema, Hessel E., defense of modern legal thought, 7; on verification, 74

Z

Zeno, on change, 84

Zoning, 95

www.ingramcontent.com/pod-product-compliance
Lightning Source LLC
Chambersburg PA
CBHW030652270326
41929CB00007B/334

* 9 7 8 1 4 6 9 6 1 3 2 5 3 *